To Dad ... 1975

From

Ex Libris...
Glenn T. Seaborg

D1457321

THE WORLD I LIVED IN

Books by George Jessel
 S' Help Me
 This Way Miss
 Elegy in Manhattan
 The Toastmaster's Guide to Public Speaking
 Halo over Hollywood

Books by John Austin
 Sex Is Big Business
 Hollywood's Unsolved Mysteries

THE WORLD I LIVED IN

GEORGE JESSEL

with John Austin

Henry Regnery Company · Chicago

Library of Congress Cataloging in Publication Data

Jessel, George Albert, 1898-
     The world I lived in.

     Includes index.
     1. Jessel, George Albert, 1898-   I. Austin,
John, 1922-   joint author.   II. Title.
     PN2287.J56A39   791.092'4 [B]   75-14166
     ISBN 0-8092-8243-7

Copyright ©1975 by George Jessel and John Austin
All rights reserved
Published by Henry Regnery Company
180 North Michigan Avenue, Chicago, Illinois 60601
Manufactured in the United States of America
Library of Congress Catalog Card Number: 75-14166
International Standard Book Number: 0-8092-8243-7

Published simultaneously in Canada by
Fitzhenry & Whiteside Limited
150 Lesmill Road
Don Mills, Ontario M3B 2T5
Canada

I have lived three days
in every twenty-four hours . . .
—Charles Baudelaire

I am as unashamed of my life as
a poodle with a pillow . . .
—George Jessel

To my dear friend
IRVING BERLIN
the genius
whose couplet from a popular song
made me tell this story of my life

"From out of the past where
forgotten things belong . . .
You keep coming back like a song. . . ."

Contents

PROLOGUE

As It Was in the Beginning . . .

I was named after a second cousin of my father's, Sir George Jessel, Master of the Rolls of Great Britain and Solicitor-General. Sir George was the first and only man of his religious beliefs, up to that time, to hold such an exalted office. (The *Encyclopaedia Britannica* will verify this fact for those who doubt it.)

None but Disraeli and Lord Reading has been so honored. My grandfather, Edward Aaron Jessel, came to America in 1835, located in California in 1849, and made and lost several fortunes during San Francisco's most explosive era, the 1850s. He was a member of Coleman's Vigilantes, the band that cleaned up the Barbary Coast outlaws by hanging and shooting twenty-two in one night.

Later, Edward Jessel went to Chicago and was known as the King of the Auctioneers, and then lost everything in the Chicago Fire. His son, my father, Joseph Aaron Jessel, had no liking for the auctioneering business. Driven by a secret yearning for the theater, he left home to become a playwright. In his thirties he wrote *La Belle Marie*, and years later became the collaborator of Hal Reade with whom he wrote several plays, including *The War Heroine* and

1

Remarkable Woman. During one of the many seasons of *La Belle Marie*, of which he was also the producer and manager, he married the star, Agnes Herndon.

When a new play for her failed, he left show business and became a traveling salesman. This was the heyday of the salesman —then called a drummer—who was as romantic a figure to the small towns as the minstrel, and much more dependable. This separation caused a divorce between my father and Agnes Herndon Jessel, and in 1897 he married the errand girl of the concern for which he worked. That girl was my mother, Charlotte Jessel.

She was thirty years his junior, yet they were in love with each other. What was good enough for my father was good enough for me—girls thirty years younger than I.

But that comes later, much later.

* * *

On April 1, 1898, my father was without employment. His young wife was heavy with child whose birth was expected any day. My parents lived in a small apartment on St. Ann's Avenue, the Bronx. Compared to the romantic life of the theater, the exploits of a traveling salesman had soon lost their appeal.

In short, my father was broke, flat broke.

He had left the theater with bitter memories, but the theater was the only thing he could turn to. A note in the weekly *Dramatic Mirror* said that the popular actress Minnie Dupree was contemplating a tour of the variety halls and was looking for a one-act play. My father wrote all through the night and was at Miss Dupree's hotel in the morning with a sketch called *Checkmate, or The Woman Who Remembered.* He sold it outright for $150. This *huge* sum, for those days, paid the expenses for the first stage of my trip around the world.

I was born on April 3, 1898, during the Spanish-American trouble, but I do not remember much about my father. I do recall that his letters were flowery and that it was always better to say "it is not light" in preference to "it is dark." The only phrase I can remember, directly addressed to me, was, "You will never become an actor as long as I live." There are some people through the years who would venture a guess that he was right. Nevertheless, I have had a hell of a lot of fun, made, spent, and lost several million dollars, met kings, presidents, prime ministers, queens, sheiks, pimps, whores, and panderers, not to mention a few gangsters, stars, and starlets.

I have been married to three beautiful women: Florence Courtney, Norma Talmadge, and Lois Andrews; and almost married to Rita Hayworth—until she confused me with someone named "Phil." That can be very disconcerting on a wedding trip to Las Vegas.

* * *

I have one daughter, Jerilynn, conceived within wedlock to Lois Andrews, and one daughter, Chrissie, conceived out of wedlock by Joan Tyler—my $200,000 baby (that's what the paternity suit cost me to defend). How, will come later. But I have made it a rule never to get laid in a beach house from that day to this.

I have another child somewhere; I believe he is in South America. David was born out of wedlock to an American entertainer I met in Paris in 1933. I have never seen him and never knew about him until five years after the fact.

* * *

My father died in 1908 and, after six months in public school, I left to go on the stage with Gus Edwards.

I have spent my life on stages all over the world ever since—from the deck of an aircraft carrier in Pearl Harbor (a frightening experience because of the size of the crowd, over 5,000), on Broadway, in London, Paris, Monte Carlo, Chicago, San Francisco, and even Peoria and Wilkes-Barre, to improvised platforms in the pouring rain in Vietnam; the day after one appearance in Vietnam, I had to jump from a burning helicopter a la John Wayne and injured my leg rather badly. (At least I was awarded the Purple Heart!)

I injured my other leg while saluting the late, great General Creighton Abrams just before he pinned the Distinguished Service Cross on my breast. Not being a military man by profession, I tried to click my heels and salute at the same time. My arm came up but my right heel missed the left and I fell rather hard. It was probably the first time in the annals of warfare that the DSO had been pinned on someone who was lying flat on his ass in the mud of a battlefield after attempting to salute a general. I still walk with a slight limp.

I have never regretted one moment of my life. There are many things I probably would have done differently were I to be given a second chance. I have always told my daughter Jerilynn, "Reach as high as you can and while I'm still able, I'll help you to reach even higher. . . ."

As we write this story of my life, I am better known throughout the God-fearing countries of the world than ever I have been before.

While I don't appear on network television too often anymore—for stepping on the toes of the little boys on Madison Avenue—my few appearances seem to "hold," and I meet people all across this land on my speaking tours who imagine they see me very often.

As I have stated many times during my career, for all its ups and downs, I am not bitter about anything because you can't do anything well when you are bitter.

My life has always been an open book with just a few of the pages stuck together. . . .

Until now.

Some people may not like what I have to say about them; they are impressions and opinions, but honest ones. Others will be pleasantly surprised at what I have to say about them. But there is one thing in my life I have never been accused of—that is lying to anyone about anything.

That credo shall be followed in this account of my life—for better or for worse.

I am now seventy-seven years old and let the chips fall where they may.

* * *

It all started in a little tailoring shop in Harlem. . . .

1

My First Partner—Walter Winchell

WHEN my father became very ill in 1907 and was unable to earn a living, my mother, little brother, and I went to live with my grandparents on her side, Simon and Caroline Schwartz on 118th Street in Harlem.

My grandfather was a tailor but his chief income was from pressing and mending clothes. Pants were pressed for ten cents, and when a customer came in he generally took them off in the shop and covered himself with his coat. For suffering this discomfort, if you will, my blind grandmother always provided him with a cup of coffee and a piece of cake, or a sandwich—sometimes even a piece of fish. No businessman, my grandfather.

I was generally asked to sing a song while the pressing was going on. I was loud enough to be heard above the hiss of the steam —something that has stood me in good stead throughout my career—I learned to project very early in life.

My baby brother, Edward Aaron Jessel, had been a premature baby and was not very strong. An epidemic of scarlet fever that had broken out in our neighborhood hit me very hard. I was delirious for five days, but on the sixth, my nurse announced that I had recovered sufficiently to warrant a plate of ice cream. When the dish was returned to the kitchen, Edward Aaron licked the plate and died a week later. He was little more than two years old at the time.

Encouraged by my pantless audience—captive, you might say—in my grandfather's shop, I once went with him to a lodge meeting. The president announced that Simon Schwartz had brought his grandson to sing and dance for the members. My debut consisted of several songs I had been singing, if it could be called such, at the tailoring shop: "Every Morning I Bring Thee Violets," "Dearie," "I'm Afraid to Go Home in the Dark," and "School Days." Most of the members were hard of hearing, and two card games and a collection for a late member's funeral started up during "Dearie." I was still undaunted.

I left the meeting to visit my mother, who, because of many injudicious investments with the local bookie, and my grandfather's penchant for feeding his customers, had taken a job as a ticket seller at the Imperial Theater on 116th Street. The family was in pretty bad shape financially. But I was determined to have my mother arrange for the manager of the theater to hear me sing.

In those days, every motion picture theater had song pluggers who would sing their latest numbers accompanied by colored slides shown on the screen. For example, during "I Dreamed in the Gloaming of You," the singer would begin the chorus and the picture would show a handsome swain looking up at the moon.

The man who owned the Imperial told me that he had hired two other boys the day before, a bit older than myself, but he said we could, perhaps, get together and he would call us the Imperial Trio. The other two boys were immediately sent for. One was an alto singer, the other a tenor. The latter was Jack Wiener, now a famed Hollywood agent who once managed my late ex-wife Lois. The alto was Walter Winchell, a handsome little guy with a fairly good voice and the heart throb of 116th Street.

The first thing we did, even before rehearsing a song, was to decide on a stage name. In those days, no matter what your name was, you called yourself something else—generally to avoid bill collectors. So, Wiener, Winchell, and Jessel became Leonard, Lawrence, and McKinley, the Imperial Trio. Because we were under sixteen, the Gerry Society* forbade our singing on the stage. Instead, we sang in the little piano pit to the accompaniment of Harry Carroll and later Phil Baker.

The popular songs of the day were "Pony Boy," "Carrie," "Meet Me Tonight in Dreamland." My solo was a song of the racetrack—with all due respect to my late mother—"I'd Rather Be the Lobster Than the Wise Guy." We did pretty well in the afternoons but the nighttime audiences resented us because the lights were put on, thus interrupting a great deal of heavy necking (and other things), which was the main reason for going to a movie in those days, particularly in that neighborhood with its lack of motels and crowded tenement bedrooms.

As a result, very often during our evening act, pickles and other assorted garnish from the local deli came flying through the air in our direction. To stop the disturbance, the management engaged a bouncer, later known as "Gyp the Blood," who was very quietly bounced himself several years later as one of the assassins of Herman Rosenthal, the Metropole Hotel gambler.

During one of our performances, the customers upstairs were decidedly disturbed by the lights that cut into their, shall we say, cuddling time. Added to that, Winchell, who was the lead singer, was missing—a song with a tenor and a baritone singing harmony without the actual melody was none too melodious. However, Gyp started his customary duties of bouncing the lovers out of the balcony. The first couple he came to was Winchell and a neighborhood girl of rather loose morals called Eva; they were locked in a passionate embrace. Because I told the theater manager of this, Winchell spent most of the rest of his life getting even with me.

The trio was fired and Clarence McKibben, the manager, decided he would have only vaudeville and no more illustrated songs. He could get a real act for what he was paying us—$12 per week, with Sunday extra at ten cents a song, which gave us $13.50 a week to split three ways. I was kept on alone at a flat $5 per week with

---

*The Gerry Society was an organization that was formed in the early 1900s for the express purpose of keeping children off the stage. No one knows of its exact origin unless it was formed by a group of jealous midgets. The Gerry Society, however, raised no objection to children selling newspapers on the street in heat, cold, rain, or snow, or from working in factories for 15¢ per hour.

my first billing in front of a theater: "It's worth 5¢ alone to hear little Georgie Jessel sing."

(About thirty years later Winchell wrote: "And it still goes." Ah, Walter, such a small, vindictive man.)

As fate would have it, the Imperial Trio met again in Tin Pan Alley two weeks later. I had gone down to learn a song that I was to sing the following Sunday in the box of the Academy of Music on Fourteenth Street. The reason for this one-day engagement was that the booking manager of the Academy had arranged for a cartoonist to do a drawing act on a tryout basis. He suggested having a kid singer in the box while the artist worked. That cartoonist was the famed Rube Goldberg.

I never fulfilled that engagement for, to celebrate our meeting, Winchell, Wiener, and I went for a hamburger at Foddington's Restaurant. The hamburger served to me had some added ingredients—matches, a little tobacco, and parts of dead cigars. Someone, apparently, had dumped the ashtrays in the meat grinder. Needless to say, I was violently ill for several days.

Before this ptomaine episode we, the Imperial Trio, had paid a visit to Gus Edwards. Gus dealt only with kids who had stage ability and he was the greatest sentimental song writer of his time. He was also producing many acts with kids, many of whom reached great heights over the years. To make an impression on Edwards, I wore long trousers, at the age of ten yet, and sang a new Irving Berlin ballad, "Yiddle on Your Fiddle." (I am sure Irving would never admit to this little ditty today.) I was also sporting a new Windsor tie, and I carried a cane and makeup box under my arm. All this was to make sure that everyone knew I was an actor and also in the hope that I would be mistaken for a midget if someone wanted to engage me without worrying about that damned Gerry Society.

Before I started to sing the Berlin "classic," I borrowed Gus's hat, which came way down over my ears. When I added a catch line of my own to the song, it caught his fancy. He took our names and addresses and I was sent for a few days later. I found myself seated in Edwards's outer office alongside a young man I had met before. He had appeared so often at the Imperial, doing imitations one week, a monologue in Yiddish the next, and the following week a

blackface minstrel act. I thought he had more *chutzpah* than anyone I had ever met before.

"What are you doing here?" he asked.

"Gus Edwards sent for me," I told him in my haughtiest, show
business manner. "What are *you* doing here?"

"I'm going to do some of my stuff for Mr. Edwards."

I was just about to tell him that I doubted if Mr. Edwards
had that much time when the door opened. He didn't give me a
chance to, though, because my nervy friend introduced himself
immediately.

"Mr. Edwards, I'm Eddie Cantor. This little fellow can tell
you about me. I would like to get in one of your new acts."

"What do you do?" Edwards asked rather cautiously.

"What do I do?" Cantor said, his eyes almost knocking Edwards down. "Such a question. I imitate June McCrea, Walter
Thompson, Walter C. Kelly, and Eddie Leonard," referring to the
top vaudeville stars of the day.

"That's very good," said Gus, a little nonplussed, "but I in-
tend producing an act called *Benches in the Park* and I don't need
any imitations, I am looking for someone to play a tramp."

"For heaven's sake," screamed Cantor, his eyes popping six
ways to glory and back again, "A tramp? I was brought up with
tramps. I play the darndest tramp you ever saw in your life."

Needless to say, we got the job(s).

Cantor immediately started his inventive mind working and
suggested that I play a baby in a carriage. He would come along
and flirt with my nurse and, to make a hit with her, he would do all
his imitations. He then invented some lines for *me* to say. He taught
me how to sock a point over. As fate would have it, the production
never materialized, but I owe a great deal to Eddie Cantor, eight
and a half years older than I. He taught me all about winning an
audience, and we were to become the greatest of friends over the
years, later to be partners and then to fight and make up, knock
each other on the stage and on radio, go on a record-breaking tour
throughout the country in the late thirties, playing sixty one-night
stands.

* * *

On that tour, we lived on a special train and only talked on the stage, venting our displeasure at each other through the audience and sending messages through our valets.

In Houston, Texas, we appeared at the old Town Auditorium, and opposite there used to be a great church. On its roof was a large electric sign reading, "Jesus Saves." A few days earlier I had heard Eddie, through his dressing room door, tell his valet that if I stopped telephoning glamour girls all over the country, I might have something to eat in my old age. When I came on stage that night to do my monologue, I told the audience:

"That's an inspiring electric sign across the street. But they should have added, 'But not like Cantor!' "

We were very close friends and had no sisters or brothers. We used to address each other as "brother" when we met and when we wrote to each other. It was that way until Eddie died many years ago.

* * *

A few days after the meeting with Eddie in Gus's office, I was hired to appear in a vaudeville act called *School Boys and Girls*. After a ten-day rehearsal, we opened at the New Brighton Casino in Brighton Beach—my first appearance in a big-time vaudeville theater. On the bill for two shows a day were, among others, Smeroff and Sonia, from the St. Petersburg ballet, Cook and Lorenz, Laddie Cliff, London's favorite boy comedian, Bedini and Arthur (for whom Cantor was working), the world-famous jugglers—it said on the playbill.

Naturally, as an eleven-year-old kid, I was awed by the majesty of these "important" acts. Adding fuel to my show business imagination, Johnny Lorenz told me many tall stories. Among them that he and his partner were getting $1,500 per week and that he had taught George M. Cohan how to dance. Had it not been for a friend of mine, Cantor, putting me straight, I believe Lorenz would have convinced me he had written Lincoln's Gettysburg Address.

My illusions were shattered when Cantor took me aside and told me not to believe anything Lorenz said. He had just loaned him a buck for dinner. Eddie, at the time, was earning $15 a week.

School Boys and Girls consisted of ten people, five girls and four boys plus the manager. Four of the girls were in their late teens, and the fifth, in her early twenties, acted as the school-teacher in the act and was the *prima donna*. Of the four boys, three were in their early twenties, and I was eleven at the time. Following the New Brighton Casino, we were booked into the Orpheum Theater in Reading, Pennsylvania. My grandfather made a special suit with long trousers and an overcoat from unclaimed apparel in his shop. My Aunt Mary packed a food hamper with enough stashed inside to feed the entire state of Pennsylvania with Delaware thrown in.

The oldest of the girls told my mother that she would personally look after me. She was my first crush. From the early morning arrival at the Folgers Hotel, I aged many years. It had been arranged beforehand that the four boys would stay together in a room that had two large beds. All of us went right to bed in order to get a few hours' rest before the opening show.

I couldn't sleep. The exhilaration of being away from home, and with people who were practically strangers, in a dingy, theatrical hotel room, kept me wide awake. I'm glad I was.

Soon, the girl who was to "take care of me," accompanied by one of the other girls, tiptoed softly into the bedroom. My bed partner was sound asleep, but both the girls talked to me very sweetly, tucked me in and closed my eyes. They tiptoed over to the other bed and got right in.

One of life's most interesting mysteries—until that time—was unfolded for me. If you've ever committed sexual acrobatics in a dingy hotel room in a squeaky bed, you know what I mean. Neither couple could establish a cadence with the other. As one couple went up, the other came down, squeak, squish, squeak, squish. It went on for about two hours, and a little pup tent was being formed in the middle of my side of the bed.

After a few days on the tour, I had become quite a problem to the troupe, who by that time were all screwing each other whenever they could get some sack time. Having been witness to the first session, I was carefully put to sleep each night with a bottle of beer spiked with a shot of cheap bourbon. To this day, I can't look a bottle of beer in the face—only whiskey.

Later, I was taken out of this act and put in the largest and most spectacular vaudeville act ever produced up to that time —Gus Edwards's Song Revue. The show had ten scenes and a cast of thirty. My part was as a member of the Newsboys Sextette with Walter Winchell as the lead singer. We broke in the act at the Hudson Theater in Union Hill, New Jersey. One of the numbers was a song satire on a play, *Alias Jimmy Valentine*, written by Wilson Mizener, the fabled character I was to meet later on during my career.

The lyricist of the Gus Edwards songs, with whom he had written *School Boys and Girls*, and many other hits, was Will D. Cobb. Most of the famous lyricists I talked to in later years were of the opinion that Cobb was the greatest lyricist America has ever known. In my opinion, only Oscar Hammerstein II could top him. But Cobb, being a sort of genius, was also a bit of an alcoholic, and when the parody of Jimmy Valentine was to be written for me, Billy was out getting mad at Schopenhauer or Nietzsche with Haig and Haig Pinch.

Fortunately, there was another young lyricist hanging around at the time with a million lyrics in his pocket. That young man was Earl Carroll, and Gus had him write the parody for me.

The revue was a sensation in Union Hill and was immediately booked the following week at Hammerstein's Victoria on Forty-second Street, the most glamorous vaudeville theater in the world at that time. No other variety theater ever presented such a range of performers as did the great impresario Oscar Hammerstein I and his Barnum-like son, Willy. Any name that found itself on the front pages would be seen in person at Hammerstein's.

When two young ladies of the town were charged with the murder of millionaire E. D. Stokes and were set free on bail, they were immediately booked into Hammerstein's as "The Shooting Stars." On the same bill was the Italian immigrant Dorando, who had failed to win the marathon race at Madison Square Garden in which he was heavily favored—and bet on. He had incurred the displeasure of every Italian on Mulberry Street.

Our engagement at Hammerstein's was of major importance. This was the show window for theatrical offerings. Only a day or two before our opening, the bane of our existence, the damned Gerry Society, notified Gus Edwards that we could not appear in

New York City on the stage. This was a real tragedy for the act, since it meant that Georgie Price, a child named Cuddles, and I would not be allowed to appear. Winchell had grown a great deal (in stature only) and he could get by.

Cuddles arrived on the scene one day when Edwards, Georgie Price, and myself passed a small hotel somewhere in the bowels of New York. Through the window of its lobby we saw a child playing with a cat. She was about three years old and her dark hair hung to the floor. Gus walked into the hotel, talked to the child's father and mother, and that afternoon when we opened the act, the first one to come on stage was this adorable child. Gus named her Cuddles for marquee purposes and she and Georgie Price were later to become famous as the child team of Cuddles and George. Cuddles eventually blossomed into beautiful womanhood and became known as Lila Lee.

A Broadway tout advised me to procure the birth certificate of an older boy for the expected onslaught of the Gerry Society inspectors. If they questioned me, the false birth certificate, added to my unusually low voice, my long trousers, and my Edwin Booth-like appearance would help me get away with it. I eventually was given a birth certificate by a considerate stagehand in the name of Imroe Kazarni. Gus, bewildered by all the palaver raised by that damned society—the sort of Ralph Nader organization of its day for the stage—accepted my plan and I was immediately put through all of Georgie Price's work in the act in case he didn't get by the inspectors.

(Many years later, Georgie was to close his own act with a satire on me.)

Louis Silvers, the musical director, put me through my paces. It looked as if I was all set, and I figured I would at least get by the first show before the *polizei* would come backstage. But I was wrong. We were notified that the underage kids were to be questioned before the show opened. That morning in April, 1910, was one of horror for me, and I never expected to go through it again. But I did, thirty years later, when I shot a man in the ass after I caught him in Norma Talmadge's bedroom after we had split up.

At 9:30 A.M. I was pacing nervously outside the stage door, my mind intent on the third degree I was to be subjected to at 10:00 A.M. Then an actor passed by who had been on the bill with us at

Proctor's Theater in Cohoes, New York, when I was with the *School Boys and Girls* act. He was also a big practical joker. I told him of my difficulties with the Gerry Society and asked his advice. He suggested that when I was being questioned by the inspector, I ask that the inquisition be hurried up because I had an appointment with my doctor due to a severe case of the clap.

This, he assured me, would fool them because they would never believe that I was only eleven years old. This was a happy thought. With my low voice, Imroe Kazarni's birth certificate, a long pair of second-hand trousers, an unlit cigar in my hand, and this very masculine affliction, it was a cinch I'd get by.

Perhaps I would have, but I, little naive dope that I was, had to help things along by asking the inspector to hurry up with his questioning because my syphilis was paining me terribly. I didn't open at Hammerstein's.

After the rest of the act had played out its run and had been a great success—even without the kids—it made the rounds of the other Percy Williams Vaudeville Theaters, and I was sneaked back into the show in Atlantic City where we closed the season.

In the meantime, Eddie Cantor had been signed by Edwards, and *Kid Kabaret* was put into rehearsal featuring Eddie Cantor and George Jessel. My mother was engaged to act as companion for the kids. Cantor played a butler in blackface, and did imitations of Eddie Leonard and Al Jolson, who was rapidly becoming an important star—and his ego was becoming just as big.

I did comedy bits with Eddie, then powdered my hair to do my imitation of David Warfield in *The Music Master*. We toured the country with this act, and in Chicago, the late Percy Hammond, the famous dramatic critic of the *Chicago Tribune*, said of me, "This little kid will have to be reckoned with a decade hence in the front rank of America's entertainers." Coming from a critic as well known as Hammond, I did not realize in my youth what a compliment he had paid me.

A few weeks later found us playing New Orleans, and I had been looking forward to this first visit to the fabled city of jazz. Not only was the weather balmy, the food different, but I was to see for the first time in my life, the famous "over the tracks" section —New Orleans' famed sporting house district. There were hundreds of cribs as well as large palaces such as Lulu White's and Jess Arlington's, replete with mirrored bedrooms and stabled with talented girls from all over the world.

We opened at the Orpheum on a Sunday night and the curtain fell at 11:00. Most of us were "over the tracks" by 11:10, and because we were sightseeing as guests of the management, we visited one of the larger houses. During the previous year, I had been learning to read and became very interested in how girls came to that sort of life. Each one, I thought, would have a sad story of white slavery and tear-jerking experiences. They were, however, the happiest group of women I had ever met until that time. Some of the older boys went upstairs for "one on the house" in exchange for theater passes. I did not. Not that I was afraid, but even then I had to have "romance" before I got laid. This idiosyncrasy of mine has been very expensive over the years. But I have adhered to it throughout my life.

But again I'm getting way ahead of myself because my adolescence was coming to an end following our return to New York from New Orleans and it is time to get on with my trip around this world.

2

Exit Adolescence–Enter Great Britain

Oᴿᴾʜᴇᴜᴍ Time'' was the most important booking for any vaudeville act in the country. The tour covered all the large cities between Chicago and the Pacific coast. This included Winnipeg, Edmonton, Regina, and Vancouver in Canada. The circuit was built and created by Morris Myerfield and Martin Beck, two Austrian immigrants. Beck started as a waiter in Chicago, then became president of the circuit and then later the owner of the Palace Theater in New York as well as the theater that still bears his name on Broadway.

For a change, they treated vaudeville with a dignity that it had never had before. The orchestras in most places included a harp and an organ. No price was too big to pay a headliner.

Kid Kabaret began a tour of the Orpheum circuit in Winnipeg. One of the other attractions on the bill was Helen Trix. Helen was born in a small town in Pennsylvania, had gone to Europe as a pianist, and had now returned to America as a typical English lady singing songs with a decidedly Mayfair accent—as though she had marbles in her mouth.

Helen was the first gentlewoman I had ever known, and I have to admit it was she who started me on my lifetime habit of reading and educating myself because of my lack of a formal education.

When the Orpheum tour ended I knew most of the "Indian Love Lyrics" by heart, as Helen used to read them to me on the long sleeper jumps through the tour. I was fourteen and terribly in love with her. She had been married to the famous Irish monologist, Frank Fogerty, but they had been divorced several years earlier. She was very sweet to me, often casting an eye upon the bulge in my trousers whenever I was near her.

On arriving in San Francisco, she held my hand and told me she would not be seeing so much of me from now on because "her man" was waiting for her. He turned out to be Jimmy Britt, the former light heavyweight champion of the world. I found myself mumbling aloud one of the poems she had taught me, "For This Is Our Wisdom."

> To love, to live, to take what fate the Gods may give
> To ask no question, to make no prayer
> Just kiss the lips and caress the hair.
> Speed passions ebb as you greet its flow
> To have, to hold and in time let go . . .

I kept repeating this for many days until one dinner time in a Kosher restaurant on Turk Street in San Francisco, Eddie Cantor said to me, "Georgie, stop crying in the noodle soup. It's weak enough as it is."

We were in the restaurant because of Cantor's impression of Al Jolson. Jolson caught the act one matinee and insisted on taking us to dinner.

Jolie came backstage to congratulate Eddie on his impressions of him, and when Cantor told him he only ate in Kosher restaurants, Jolie said he knew just the place. Jolson knew everything about San Francisco for he had lived there for many, many years and was very, very popular. In fact, Jolie died while in San Francisco.

With Al and Cantor swapping gags, everyone in the restaurant eventually gathered around the table. One man asked if he could sit down for a moment and then immediately did so without waiting for an invitation.

"I have a brother who had been trying to be a writer for the theater but he's now gone into politics."

Out of my childish politeness (and interest) because everyone else was ignoring the stranger, I replied, "Who might that be?"

"His name is Meyer Finkelstein. I'm his brother Morris, and we were born in Russia. But," the stranger went on wistfully, "he recently wrote me that he has gone into world politics and is now living in Russia again. He has changed his name to Maxim Litvinoff. But me—I'm just a tailor and cleaner from Seattle."

Many years later I was to meet Maxim Litvinoff when he became the Soviet ambassador to the United States soon after Franklin Delano Roosevelt recognized the Red regime immediately after taking office in 1932.

As for Al Jolson, I will have a lot to say about him in the following chapters.

I was very lovesick for the next few days after Helen joined Britt at the St. Francis Hotel. The elder and wiser Cantor told me: "Forget about such things. Only your career matters. In our work you will meet the most beautiful women in the world." How right he turned out to be.

"And besides," said Cantor, "we must watch this fellow who is on the bill with us, Will Rogers. Only two years ago he was doing a roping act with a trained horse, and now [1913] all he does is talk, chew gum, and do tricks with a rope, and he's getting $1,000 a week."

We set our sights on that astronomical figure, never dreaming we would someday be earning that kind of money and much more ourselves.

About that time, I reached the awkward stage, a period that affects kids in show business more than kids not in public life. I was growing fast and my voice was changing. Little whiskers were commencing to sprout and I felt awful. Consequently it affected my work, so much so that when we came back to New York for an engagement at Hammerstein's, Sime Silverman, editor and publisher of *Variety*, the show business bible, wisely though murderously wrote of me as follows:

"Georgie Jessel is growing and with the passing of his cuteness it is hoped that he will perforce make it up with ability."

It was a far cry from what Percy Hammond had written a year or two earlier. I vowed that I would show him.

After we returned to New York, *Kid Kabaret* finished its run. It was a good thing because I was outgrowing all my clothes and my grandfather had to lengthen everything I owned.

Cantor found a partner called Kessler who had arranged for them to go to London, for a tour of England. The day before they sailed, Eddie married Ida, the wife he talked about on his radio show for years until you nearly went crazy. As they sailed on the *Aquitania* for London and their honeymoon, I said goodbye sadly at the pier. Our hopes of becoming a famous team were over as far as I was concerned.

I was cutting myself to pieces every day shaving, and I liked girls more than ever, only they didn't like me so much. I had a three-day job in a motion picture, a two-reeler, *The Widow at the Races*, in which I played Alphonse of "Alphonse and Gaston," a famous comic strip of the day.

They were two bogus Frenchmen—is there any other kind?—with high hats, mustaches, and goatees. The first day's shooting was to be a sequence off Sheepshead Bay in a rowboat that was to be turned over. I had been asked when I came in for the job whether or not I could swim; five dollars a day was five dollars a day, so I said yes. That, of course, was a lie. When the boat did turn over, I lost my glued-on whiskers and was almost drowned.

I have had an aversion to rowboats ever since.

Hustling for a buck, I became friendly with another Gus Edwards actor, Lou Edwards—no relation. He couldn't talk much, but, boy, could he dance. We rehearsed like crazy and put on an act, *Two Patches from a Crazy Quilt*, by Joe Laurie, Jr. We broke in the act in theaters very much resembling men's rooms in railroad stations and had a tough time. There was a circuit called "The Sheedy Time." (It should have been spelled "Shitty.") It consisted of theaters through upper New England and Nova Scotia, if you can imagine, and we were hired for the circuit. The only good things in the act were Lou's dance and my imitation of Charlie Chaplin, who was, by then, becoming very popular as the Little Tramp.

I'll never forget the opening in Gloucester, Massachusetts, in the dead of winter at a little theater at the end of a pier. The dressing rooms were afloat with sea water and we had to put boards and boxes on the floor to make up and dress. I had a start one night when a fish jumped out between the boards, looked around and went back under. It was a "tough time," all right.

On the bill was an act called *Too Much Mustard*, the leading lady of which was a girl called Mabel. She had been in burlesque and appeared in tights at the end of the act. And I mean tights so every curve from her boobs to her pubic mound was outlined. She had long black hair, and eyes that made me bone up on the "Indian Love Lyrics."

We had a big affair, water or no water, in the dressing room. We managed to make out with Mabel sitting on an orange crate, her feet awash, with my knees between them. Several times, at the crucial moment, a fish would take a bite out of my knee or my leg if one or the other happened to slip off the floor board.

When we left Gloucester for Boston, Mabel sorrowfully told me there would be no assignation at the hotel there for us because the guy who owned the act, an Englishman, was stuck on her and was coming up to see her that night.

I raised hell. The hotel room was something I had been looking forward to, a night of heaven in comparison to a quick piece in a dressing room afloat with half of Cape Cod Bay, or whatever it was, not to mention call boys knocking on the door and a thousand other interruptions not conducive to romance.

No, I would not stand for this guy coming up and keeping me away from Mabel. I made quite a scene.

But Mabel appeased me by promising that she would have her boyfriend book me and Edwards into a London theater. It turned out that her paramour was an important person in theatrical circles in England, which was then embroiled in her first conflict with Germany.

"But what if he doesn't like our act?" I asked innocently, but practically.

"Don't worry, I'll put it over. You'd be surprised what you can do during that crucial moment in bed, Georgie."

She did, but how and when and at what moment, I never asked.

Jessel and Edwards—or was it Edwards and Jessel? I forget —jumped from the Beacon Theater in Boston—a ten-cent vaudeville theater—to the Victoria Palace in London with an eight-week booking at $250 per week, split two ways. I was in the big time! We were only earning $75 a week between us at the time, when we could get it, and in theaters such as the one on the end of that damn pier. Now we were booked into one of the finest variety theaters in the world—London's Victoria Palace. And the man who booked us had never seen our act. That will give you an idea of how adroit Mabel was between the sheets, even better than while astraddle an orange crate, I imagine.

World War I was in its second year, and the great city of London was in complete darkness from the blackout. The Zeppelin raids had begun, and there were no porters at Waterloo Station when we arrived on the boat train from Southampton.

We arrived at 4:30 A.M. and had to carry our own trunks from the baggage car. Because of the hour, we booked ourselves into a room at the station hotel, which, I believe, is still renting the same rooms sixty years later.

"You and your goddamned Indian Love Lyrics," Edwards said, rather scathingly, as we devoured a meal of tea, toast, and marmalade—no butter—our first in nearly six hours.

I felt it more prudent to make no comment.

Lou and I felt a little better after a rest, and in the morning we took a bus ride to see the sights of London and to acquaint ourselves with the layout of this great city, land of my esteemed ancestors. It has always amazed me about the British, not only in the First World War but in the Second as well, as to the way they "carry on regardless." Here they were engaged in a brutal, bloody struggle with the Kaiser's forces and during the day everything appeared to be perfectly normal. Buses and taxis filled the streets, top-hatted and striped-trousered messengers were delivering whatever they had to deliver, and the gilded lords and ladies of London were driving, or being driven, around the streets of London in their huge Daimlers and Rolls-Royces. The same was true during World War II. You never really realized there was a war going on until the blackout started at dusk.

Naturally, our bus ride took us past Buckingham Palace, and

if I had dreamed then that I, a struggling Jewish singer and comedian from Harlem, forty-odd years later would be dancing with a
former mistress of this beautiful palace, I would have committed
myself to an institution then and there.

And if anyone had ever told me that I would be entertaining
that royal family forty-odd years later at the *same* theater, the Victoria Palace, into which Lou and I were booked, I would have had
them committed as well.

When Lou and I finally arrived at the theater to look it over
and meet the stage manager, his only advice to us was to be careful
of using certain words and phrases that did not have the same
meaning in England as they did in the U.S.A. This was wasting time
since we had no jokes with any of the words he mentioned. He then
told us of a hotel off Leicester Square that was frequented by
American variety acts that were not terribly important—such as
Jessel and Edwards.

The Province turned out to be nothing more than a large pub
with just a few rooms upstairs. The bar was a new and strange sight
to me. I had never seen lady bartenders, nor had I ever known
there were three classes of rooms in English pubs—first, second,
and third. Very respectable people went into these bars, sure to
find people of their own station in life. The old British class system,
of course.

The first Americans we bumped into were members of an act
called the Fruit Pickers. They were appearing in one of the London
music halls packing oranges, grapefruit, and lemons into boxes
with amazing rapidity. Naturally, my mind wandered back to
Mabel's orange crate in her dressing room on the pier.

The Fruit Pickers were a great hit in London, the English
being pretty slow in such things. Edwards and I made close friends
of this act. It turned out they were farm people from the west and
had been put into vaudeville after winning the orange-packing
prize at a county fair.

They immediately did their best to show us the ropes and how
to count English money. One of the boys explained to us that a sixpence was actually twelve cents in American money and a shilling
was only a quarter. (That was when the pound was worth five dollars.) He rendered this intelligence as though it were the second-act
closing of a melodrama.

After listening to the miracle of the sixpence for the fourth time, I found myself talking to one of the girls in the act. My pecker was bulging beneath my pants once again because she was a very lovely young thing, full bosomed and with a beautiful ass. After a drink or two and a little walk around Leicester Square, we strangely enough found ourselves in her room. At least I thought it was her room.

The season was late in June and it was one of the warmest nights London had known for years. Since the shades had to be drawn because of the Zeppelin raids, it became so warm that she stripped down and donned a Chinese kimono.

Suddenly, just as I started to remove my pants, there was a great commotion in the halls and much knocking on doors. Two Zeppelins were flying over London and the antiaircraft guns started firing.

We both started to dress but were interrupted by a loud knock on the door and a man's voice yelling: "Honey, come down to the cellar."

"I'll be right down," she answered, rather nervously I thought at the time.

As I rushed to go with her, she whispered, "You come later. That's my husband!"

I never got a chance to come with her or down to the cellar later because in the excitement she put the light out, rushed out the door and locked it. I managed to escape through a window and into another room, packed my things, wrote a note for Lou explaining the situation, and left. I was damned if I wanted to face an irate husband at my age. There was no telling what this farmer would do if he learned I was compromising his wife. They used an axe in their act to open and close the orange crates, and I did not want my first trip to London to start *and* finish because of an orange crate.

I wandered out into the street just in time to see a Zeppelin hit by antiaircraft fire and explode. It was quite a sight for a young man then only fifteen years old, but I aged twenty years, though, before I checked into the Strand Palace Hotel on the Strand, a modern hotel lacking only steam heat. It's still there today and probably still without steam heat. But room and breakfast was less than two dollars—six shillings and sixpence to be precise. Lou joined me in the morning and I promised him there would be no more screwing around with married (or unmarried) women for the rest of our stay abroad—unless he was in on it to keep me out of trouble.

Lou and I attended the dress rehearsal with the lead sheets of a new song we had grabbed just before leaving New York. We were told "Hello, Hawaii" was fresh from the writer, and we thought we would have something new for our act at least musically. When we arrived backstage we heard the refrain coming from the footlights and discovered that Beatie and Babs, two very popular British kids, were rehearsing it. Our boat hadn't been fast enough. The headliner of the bill, however, was the great American star, Jack Norworth. He had been a great success in London and had migrated there after several unhappy and expensive marriages at home, including one to the famed Nora Bayes.

* * *

Jack's romance and marriage to Nora was immortalized in the film *Shine on, Harvest Moon*, the song Norworth wrote and made famous. Starring as Norworth was Dennis Morgan and Ann Sheridan as Nora Bayes. The film was a tremendous hit when it was released by Warner Brothers in 1944.

It still plays occasionally on the late, late show and was a fairly accurate portrayal of their few stormy years together.

* * *

As the top of the bill, Jack arranged for *us* to sing "Hello, Hawaii," and we became great friends, a friendship that existed until his death about twenty-odd years ago.

Norworth's reputation as a singer and songwriter, as well as an all-around good guy, drew me to his dressing room continuously. He regaled me with many stories of the theater and his own love life, which was lusty to say the least. He tried to impress upon me the fact that when a man reaches a certain age, *affairs d'amour* lose their importance. This was the only thing Jack ever told me that turned out, as far as I am concerned, pure balderdash. But as far as Jack was concerned at the time, he was through with the stuff. A week later he eloped to Scotland's Gretna Green with a twenty-year-old chorus girl.

Even to this day I have never forgotten the fascination I had listening to Jack at that time, watching him put on his immaculate evening clothes—while chewing a great wad of tobacco. It also turned out that, as a boy, Jack Norworth had been a sailor on the same ship Lou and I had sailed to England aboard, the S.S. *St. Paul.*

Two Patches from a Crazy Quilt did fairly well at the Victoria Palace—why, I don't know. Chaplin was still unknown in his native land, and I had to drop my imitation of him. The only thing we could depend on to save us from raw vegetables from the audience was the eccentric dance that Lou did while I sang in the background. It made the "act." After London we were booked into the very depressing mill town of Leeds in Yorkshire. We flopped miserably. Then it was on to Newcastle where we perished altogether and were taken off the bill the second day. At least we were paid for the week.

President Woodrow Wilson, in one of his more pacifist speeches, had come out at the time about America being too proud to fight. One of the many letters the theater received panning our act said, "If America is too proud to fight, they certainly ought to feel greater shame in sending such an act as Jessel and Edwards." In the pans, I got the top billing; in the raves, Edwards did.

They tried us in a few more cities—Manchester, Bristol, and Taunton—but it was no good. Only cosmopolitan London would have us at all, and we played two or three dates in the smaller music halls around London such as Shepherd's Bush. One of them was the Shoreditch Empire, a little theater in a district similar to New York's (then) Bowery. I was singing a Yiddish dialect song, "Nathan," which particularly pleased this audience. After the second show, all they wanted was "Nathan," and they would sing the chorus with me. On the strength of that we were booked the following week into Dublin, Ireland, if you can imagine.

We landed in Dublin on a very grim morning as Irish Rebellion Number 3,486 had already started. Some of the lads had playfully blown up the main post office for the umpteenth time. The ship's porter recommended a small hotel called the Granville House. While we were being shown our room I noticed that the curtains had a few holes in them. Naively, I inquired about it.

"Do you have moths or rather large mosquitoes?"

"No," the Irish landlady replied, rather seriously, "neither. There were some English officers staying in here only yesterday, and they stuck their heads out the window and some lads in the street started shooting at them. But it's all right now; they've moved to a room in the back of the house."

I gingerly inquired if the same accommodation in "the back of the house" was still available. When told it was not, I made a mental note not to look out that particular window.

I met these same officers later in the week and they told me they were interested in playing poker. They had only played it once or twice and thought it was "a jolly good game." I taught them all I knew about it, and when I left Dublin I had exactly sixpence in my pocket, twelve cents. Dublin was the end of *Two Patches from a Crazy Quilt* and the Jessel bankroll.

Lou, in the meantime, had sent for his American sweetheart, Betty Washington, a fine violinist. She had arrived in London and had opened in one of the London theaters where she made quite a success of her act. Lou had received an offer to do his eccentric dance act in one of the editions of the musical play, *The Bing Boys*, which was a great success in London and starred George Robey. The great song hit from the show was "If You Were the Only Girl in the World," which was written by Nat Ayer, a kid from our own Tin Pan Alley. Edwards and I parted the best of friends, and he advised me to forget about the "Indian Love Lyrics" from then on.

That day I walked around London trying to figure a way to get back home. I was flat broke, but even if I had some money, getting back would be quite a problem. The Germans had just declared ruthless submarine warfare and started sinking everything they could hit, including lifeboats from disabled liners. They always were compassionate people—and always, it seems, decadent.

My first try for a touch was backstage at the Queens Theater where *Potash and Perlmutter in Society* was playing with a full American cast. (It should be pointed out that most British male performers of military age were in the army or navy at the time, and in order to keep the British theater alive, it was mostly peopled by American performers.) I visited Lee Kohlmar and found him in an extremely happy mood. It was his son's ninth birthday.

"Here's his picture," he said, rather proudly. "And we call

him Freddy. . . ." Later, Fred Kohlmar became one of the top
producers at Paramount Pictures in Hollywood.

Thanks to Freddy's birthday, I left Liverpool two days later
on the *Baltic*, a camouflaged English vessel. It had made three
starts that week and turned back because of the U-boats. There
were exactly thirteen passengers aboard this 20,000-ton liner,
which had to go to New York to take on supplies for the be-
leaguered island. Eleven of those thirteen were Welsh seamen who
were going to New York to pick up another ship; the remaining two
were myself and a deported lunatic who immediately disappeared
when we got on board. The *Baltic*'s run from Liverpool to New
York was not quite nine days in normal times. I went to my cabin in
the bowels of the ship and was immediately summoned topside by
the purser and issued a life jacket. We were asked to draw lots as to
who would be in charge of the crackers and water—that is, of
course, if we were compelled to go over the side. With my usual
umglick, I chose the lucky number. At least I knew I would eat if
ever I had to sit in another damn rowboat—my mind casting itself
back to that two-reel short I had made before coming to London. I
never did have a chance to find out what would have happened to
me if one of those giant Welsh sailors had asked for a cracker and I
would have had to say no!

When I awoke the next morning I found we were back in
Liverpool. The subs were lurking too near shore, and we had to
come back during the night. We started again and this time kept
going. I made friends with the radio operator because I couldn't
understand what the Welsh seamen were talking about at meal-
time. While we were talking one afternoon, he received a message
that the *Laconia*, an English ship very close to us, had been hit. We
immediately changed our course, and fourteen days later were still
at sea without even an island in sight. I was beginning to believe we
were going to New York via South America and Australia. This was
March and the sea was rough as hell.

One night, as I heroically started to have dinner with my
stomach churning, I managed to understand one of the Welsh
sailors and his conversation.

"Aye, Tom, one of the stewards told me it was so rough on the
last trip over that while he was serving dinner he got sick right in
the bowl of potatoes."

"Aye," said Tom slyly, eyeing me. "What did they do about it?"

"They had to mash them."

I went right back to my cabin, but I did use that later on one of my radio shows.

At the end of an unbelievable seventeen and a half days we arrived at the Fourteenth Street pier. Because of wartime conditions, there was no way of notifying my mother or grandfather as to when I would arrive or on which ship. It was around ten o'clock at night, and I rushed to the nearest telephone and called my house. My grandfather answered the telephone.

"Hello, grandpa. This is Georgie. I just got in."

Grandpa's hearing, I discovered, had gone a little queer.

"Who is this?"

"Georgie, grandpa. George. Your grandson. I'll be home in half an hour."

"Oh," the old man replied. "You know Georgie? We don't expect him home for a few days yet, but if you leave your name I'll tell him you called."

"No, grandpa," I shrieked, "this *is* George. Tell mama and grandma I feel fine and I'll be home in a few minutes."

"Yes, I'll tell Georgie. He'll be glad to see you, too."

It was this conversation that eventually led to my famous *Hello, Mama* telephone calls act later on in my career on radio and the stage.

I arrived home to beer and fried oyster sandwiches, a *goy* delicacy. They were served on the quiet, as my grandmother would never allow such things in the house. But grandpa loved them, and if there was any trouble, he said he would take it up with Moses later on.

Meanwhile, I couldn't wait to get down to Broadway the next day and get my career going again—and get some money in my pocket.

3

The War Years on Broadway

ALL through the night I told my mother and grandparents about my experiences in England and Ireland. I had twenty dollars left from the borrowed money, an English cap and a monocle, if you please. I still wear one today—not for effect, from necessity.

I started to make the rounds of all the Broadway theaters.

What a year 1917 was for Broadway. It has never been surpassed in my opinion. The Winter Garden had the *Show of Wonders* and a Sunday night concert with Al Jolson; the Century Theater, a Dillingham-Ziegfeld production, *The Century Girl*, with Elsie Janis. Henry Miller was in *The Great Divide*; the Gaiety Theater (closed in 1942 for showing naked women in dirty sketches) was then housing the wholesome American play *Turn to the Right*. Maude Adams was in a revival of the English play *Kiss for Cinderella*, and George Arliss was appearing in another British import, *The Professor's Love Story*. Jane Cowl was in *Lilac Time*, and the headliner at the Palace was Nat C. Goodwin, whom George M. Cohan called "America's greatest actor."

After two or three weeks of meeting people from Forty-second Street to Forty-eighth Street on Broadway, telling gags to actors in their hotels, in their dressing rooms, and in restaurants while cadging free meals, there was still no prospect of any work. I was exempt from the draft because I supported my mother and grandparents. I had almost outgrown my awkward age, but not entirely. This hampered my career, since the wisecracking and sophisticated type of gag that I was telling with great effect off the stage would not serve me before an audience. I would be just a fresh kid. I might poke fun, among the gang, at Al Jolson (who was then the Toast of the Country) or Raymond Hitchcock. But I was without authority or stature to do so before the public.

A prominent vaudevillian, Henry Bergman, of the team of Clark and Bergman, took a great, fatherly interest in me and warned me that I must get to work. I couldn't go on being a dressing room clown and making no money for my trouble. He called my attention to a newspaper column written by S. Jay Kaufman. This was the first of the Broadway "gossip" columns, "Round The Town." Winchell was later to latch onto this idea and make a business of it. The item about me read: "Georgie Jessel is now an offstage little clown whom the stars have around for laughs."

Bergman was appearing at the Winter Garden, and I spent the evenings with him in his dressing room, running errands and acting as a companion to some of the showgirls, especially when they were going out with some "John" and didn't want to go to bed with them. One of these girls was the famous beauty, Jessie Reed, a titian-haired lovely who was later to be glorified by Florenz Ziegfeld. She created a sensation at a party one night when she danced every dance with a future King of England, the Prince of Wales, later Edward VIII, who eventually abdicated for the love of another American, Bessie Wallis Warfield-Simpson. Broadway was aghast at the rumors that the Prince was very inadequate sexually—too small for normal relations, the rumor went—but loved being around beautiful and glamorous women to make up for it.

Through that friendship with the Winter Garden showgirls, and the favors I did them (and they reciprocated with their female charms once in a while), I also became the constant companion of the stage manager of the Winter Garden, Zeke Colvin. I used to watch Jolson's Sunday night concerts because I hadn't seen him work before, and it was fascinating. He was a master on the stage. I later found him completely different offstage when I got to know him better.

I made great friends with Stanley Sharpe, the manager of the Winter Garden, who was also the personal manager of the lovely young Marilyn Miller. Even in her teens she was far up the ladder on her climb to eventual stardom. She was on tour in a Shubert extravaganza, and one Sunday she came into New York, as did most performers of importance in the stage and musical-comedy world, making the train jump from Buffalo or Pittsburgh to "catch Jolie" at one of his famed Sunday night concerts. Jolson would appear around 10:00 P.M. following eight or nine much less talented acts—Jolie would have it no other way—and stay on until at least midnight.

My eyes were usually fastened on Marilyn who sat in one of the boxes over the stage. Even while King Al was tearing his guts out on the Winter Garden runway about his relatives in Dixie, my mind was playing with such thoughts as Marilyn getting stuck on me and telling the Shuberts, in reverse casting couch tradition, "Either Georgie is the principal comedian in my new show or I will tear up my contract. . . ."

Sharpe introduced me to her. I was as flustered and speechless as anyone could be. Following the performance, Sharpe, Marilyn, and I walked to her apartment on Fifty-fourth Street. Sharpe went upstairs to confer with Marilyn and her mother, and I was told to go home.

Only I didn't. I waited until Sharpe came down and went away about one o'clock in the morning. I started to serenade Marilyn, who was five floors up from the street. I had recently read *Romeo and Juliet*. Marilyn must have sensed the serenade was for her immediately because hers was the first window to open. She laughed, and we began a conversation in which I can still remember saying, "How do you like your Broadway Romeo?"

She was just about to answer when her mother came to the window and shooed me away. I didn't go until a few moments later when Sharpe, whom her mother had telephoned at the start of the ruckus, came back. That was the end of the balcony scene. I soon found out, however, that Marilyn's show was playing New Haven and Providence the next week. Early in the morning, I awakened my friend, Henry Bergman, to tell him how much in love I was.

"If only I had some money, Henry, I could go to Providence and New Haven and continue my pursuit at closer range than a fifth floor window on East Fifty-fourth Street."

Henry thought it was a great idea.

"It would be good for you to be inspired by such a romance, even if nothing comes of it. Perhaps it will encourage you to get some work for yourself."

He had an idea for an act that he and Sam Lewis would write for me. It was to be called *A Ray of Sunshine*. He gave me some money as well as a discarded tuxedo, which my grandfather hastily whipped into size for me. I left for Providence with my heart churning and registered at the Crown Hotel, where the cast—and Marilyn—was staying.

I quickly looked into the dining room, but only Eugene and Willie Howard were seated at one of the tables. Willie was the star comedian in Marilyn's show. He and Gene liked me and saw me first. Gene nudged Willie with the remark, "Here comes that crazy kid with the monocle."

Willie put down his racing form and called me over. I talked to them, told them some new stories from Broadway, but all the while with my monocled eye on the door. Soon, Marilyn came in, but her mother was with her, as well as her stepfather and two Yale-type college boys. This I did not like, but she did recognize my presence with a smile. That night the Howards took me backstage. I waited until I got the chance to say hello to her. While I held her hand for a moment, I asked her if she would take supper with me after the show. She laughed and said that she didn't think so but I might call her.

I waited in the lobby of the hotel until she and her entourage returned to her suite and called immediately. No, she couldn't see me, and I couldn't come up for a minute.

"I am going to have a light supper sent up and then go to bed . . . and you should do the same," she told me, rather firmly.

But, like the time I was undaunted when the card game and funeral collections were going on during my professional debut at my grandfather's lodge, it was a simple matter to arrange something with the room service waiter.

I tipped him a two-dollar bill, told him I was an old friend of the Millers, and borrowed his coat and apron. A few quick touches with an eyebrow pencil added a French mustache to the "disguise."

I served the supper and, oh, how Marilyn laughed. The waiter's makeup fooled her mother until I got down on my knees, à la Jolie, and said, "I love you," all the while trying to pour her coffee.

That was the end, and Mrs. Miller ordered me to leave the room. In defense of my action I fervently quoted from those damn "Indian Love Lyrics" again, but this time it didn't work:

> Forgive me for I am young
> and youth is a plea
> to cancel a thousand lies
> and a thousand nights of sin.

As I made my exit with a trayful of dishes, I tripped and fell. This cost me another three dollars. In the lobby I bemoaned my fate, which was not only playing havoc with my heart but playing holy hell with my bankroll. Of the fifty dollars Henry had loaned me, there were only thirty-four dollars left.

I soon discovered there was a crap game in one of the actor's rooms. I had known of such games at the Winter Garden; sometimes a thousand dollars could be won in a very short time if the dice were hot. Here, I thought, is my opportunity to win enough and buy Marilyn some expensive gift. That would show her mother what kind of a guy I was. I found out, however, as I had in Dublin many months before, that you never win in gambling when you really need the money. The fellow with the biggest bankroll usually winds up the winner. The eight I tried to make that night never showed. I was broke, but I got a laugh for my exit line:

"Gentlemen, I understand there hasn't been an eight made in New England since Paul Revere broke the track record." In my anxiety to get out while they were still laughing, I ripped my coat on the door. But I did follow the old stage edict: "Always leave 'em laughing."

I passed Marilyn's room again, thinking perhaps the door might open and that I might steal some tiny glimpse of her again. But no. . . .

At the cigar stand in the lobby I met Sam Hearn—the famed Schlepperman. I had known him during my Gus Edwards days, and he had helped me with my imitations of David Warfield. Sam gave me my train fare back home.

This experience was of *some* value to me . . . for I made up my mind then and there—as Henry Bergman hoped I would—to get back on the stage immediately and try to make a hit. My *schlepping* days were over as far as I was concerned.

A few weeks later I opened in *A Ray of Sunshine* with Bergman's little niece Minna Marlin. I played the part of a nut who believed he was George Washington and lived in a tree. The setting was a woodland scene, and little Minna played the part of a kid dressed as Little Red Riding Hood on her way home from a party.

This was a whimsical playlet to which I had added a song or two. It opened in a break-in theater in Jamaica and was a hit almost immediately. As a result, we were booked into the Keith-Colonial at Sixty-second Street and Broadway. But the gallery of the Colonial was known for its toughness. Dramatic sketches, recitations, anything genteel that lasted over two or three minutes brought forth catcalls and penny throwing reminiscent of the Imperial Theater deli garnish of my days with the Imperial Trio. We were treated to exactly that reception at the opening matinee. When I returned to the theater, our act had been cancelled and *A Ray of Sunshine* with its whimsy and its woodland setting was packed up and sent to the storehouse.

The following night I was back at my old stand at the Winter Garden, but no one paid much attention to me. I wasn't very funny following my disaster of the night before. Only Henry Bergman told me not to worry.

"Nothing will stop you," he said. This made me feel a little better, but I felt I didn't have a chance in show business. A few days later, however, an act at Keith's Riverside failed to show up for their performance, and, because no one else was around, the booking office sent me up to hold the stage for five or six minutes. This was the first opportunity at ad-libbing I had ever had. I was scared out of my wits.

I stayed on for sixteen minutes and was a big hit. When I came off, I couldn't remember one thing I had said. This experience gave me the idea to try a single act. Through Eddie Cantor I arranged an appointment with his manager, Max Hart, who at that time directed the theatrical destinies of Will Rogers, Frank Finney, and Bernard Granville, and had just made a deal that brought Cantor to Broadway stardom. Hart was very kind to me and told me I needed a tremendous amount of development. He handled only comedians who could get big money immediately. Since all the vaudeville managers knew me as a Gus Edwards kid, I must immediately change my name.

"You're too young in appearance for the jokes you are telling, kid," he said pontifically. "You must get some heavy facial make-up. Blackface. That's it! That's what you must do!"

It appeared that Hart, because of the success of Finney and Cantor, wanted all his comedians to black up. In fact, years later, I said to him, "Max, you won't be happy until you get up some morning and everyone is blacked up except you."

Anyway, I refused to black up. I made my next appearance on the stage as a clown with a white face under the name of George W. Grant. This was also a nothing, and a week later Hart changed my name again and I appeared with another kind of makeup. Hart naturally started to lose interest. Finally, after waiting to see him in his office for about two hours, he raised hell with me. I was a stubborn cuss.

"You're not giving enough thought to your work, Georgie. Besides that you stayed up until all hours waiting for Frances White."

Frances was appearing in the Ziegfeld Midnight Frolic, and I was in love again. The detrimental mention of that fair lady was the end of my association with Max Hart.

"All right, Mr. Hart, I will leave your management and be George Jessel again. And the next young fellow who comes up to see you, why not call him Lionel Fellowcraft and have him black up not only on the stage but on the street?"

An hour later my managers were Rose and Curtis. I was able to get into their good graces at once. That was on April 6, 1917, when war was declared on Germany. Since I had just returned from abroad, and my range of conversation interested my new managers, they kept me with them the entire evening. The actual mood of America at the time of the declaration of war was hard to estimate. There was no radio in those days. The fast transcontinental airplane was several years in the future. There was no personality like F.D.R.'s to make the "man in the street" realize what it was all about, or even make him care to, instead he had to rely on the press. Wilson, I suppose, was a good man, but it seemed that only the carriage trade and Nicholas Murray Butler understood him. I sure as hell didn't.

But it was time for me to get to work—for my new managers . . . . The future looked a little brighter . . . .

4

The War Is Over

THE night of the armistice of the War to End All Wars, I was in a small delicatessen on Seventy-second Street and Broadway. I had come to get some sandwiches for Fannie Brice, who had befriended me, and her entourage.

I returned to Fannie's with a sackful of goodies to find that Arnold Rothstein had arrived. Many people thought Rothstein was a great gambler; he was a percentage player and he never made a bet on anything unless he had a tremendous, almost sure thing advantage, as he did in the Chicago White Sox scandal a few years later.

Another distinguished looking gentleman to whom I was introduced was Nicky Arnstein, Fannie's husband at the time. Nicky was later to be accused of being the mastermind of a great bond robbery. "If Nicky ever went out to steal anything," Fannie told me later, "he would have come back empty-handed, and somebody would have copped his watch."

I can only say that Nicky was a man of infinite charm, good manners, and excellent taste. But the gay spirit of that armistice night celebration was Ann Pennington, the girl of the dimpled knees and lovely dark tresses. Naturally, I fell in love with her.

Penny, as she was known, had made a big hit with Fannie and Eddie Cantor in the Ziegfeld Follies. I flirted with her but got no encouragement, but she did accept an invitation to come up to Mt. Vernon the following week to see my act and give me some pointers. Those pointers really put me down—but for my own benefit I will have to admit.

"You're aping Eddie [Cantor] too much," were her first words after seeing the matinee. "Try to act on stage as naturally as you do off, like you did in Fannie's apartment telling us all those gags."

I listened because I was in love again and took her advice to heart. But then another vaudevillian, Al White, talked to me at great length. He started with the same old story I had heard so many times before.

"Your stuff is too smart. If you could tell your gags as if they were things you had heard instead of things you had made up, the audience would believe you and laugh."

"Why not come out on the stage," continued Al, "and call up your mother or someone at home and tell these things to them . . . ?"

It was then that that telephone conversation I had had with grandpa on my return from Europe hit me like a bell. That night I arranged with the stage manager to have the prop man hand me a telephone, and I carried out Al's (and Penny's) suggestions. But those wisecracking gags I had been doing most of my professional life did not sound to the audience (or me) like the kind of things a boy would say to his mother. In the middle of the monologue —youth has no fear on the stage or anywhere else—I dropped the wisecracking routine when I realized I wasn't going down too well. I just started to talk about homey things. I changed my act in mid-stage, so to speak.

"Listen, mama, tell the landlord it's only a few weeks now . . ." a conversation the audience could *relate* to. This intimate and natural conversation went over very well. I did the same act for over twenty years, still doing it once in a while by request of those who can remember it. In collaboration with Sam Carlton, I wrote over one thousand pages of these *Hello, Mama* conversations.

A week later, and still flushed with success, I was in Reisenweber's, and I saw a girl who was to become the first love of my life. She was sitting at a table with music publisher Henry Waterson. During the course of the evening, the lights went out because of a short circuit. But I could still see her eyes in the candlelight. She was Florence Courtney of the Courtney Sisters, an act that sang popular songs in harmony and that was a great attraction to vaudeville theaters across the country.

We were to meet again a few days later in Pittsburgh. They were headliners at the big-time theater, the Davis, while I was doing my *schtick* at the second-ranking vaude house, the Sheridan Square Theater across town. Because I was doing three and four shows a day, I could not make the Davis until the last night when I was to catch a train to Johnstown. I stopped for a sandwich at Klein's because I had been told by Joe Klein, a close friend and a man prominent in Pittsburgh theatrical circles, that he was bringing Florence and her sister Fay there for supper after their show. Immediately after we met—formally—I discovered by probing discreetly that her train was leaving for New York at 2:00 A.M. Since I could catch a train for Johnstown at almost any hour, I propositioned her.

"Why don't we take a drive together and I can drop you at the station in time for your train?"

Florence looked at me rather nervously with a glance over her shoulder to where Fay was sitting with Joe. "All right, I will," she whispered. "But you leave first because Fay objects to my going out with actors. And she particularly doesn't like young actors who have no time for serious thoughts," she laughed, quietly.

I made a quiet getaway, hired a limousine, and off we went for an hour's drive. I discovered, away from the café crowd, that Florence had a low, vibrant voice with a slight trace of the South; also, that she had been unhappily married for a short time to pianist Mike Bernard (of the Bernard and Sidney Phillips act) and had divorced him less than a year later. She had then gone with a man she had been terribly fond of, the booking manager of the Loews Circuit in New York, Joe Schenck. Joe was about to marry Norma Talmadge, and by a strange coincidence, fate or what have you, I later married Norma. But we'll go into that romance later on. Joe was also to be responsible for the happiest and most productive ten years of my life two decades later.

I told Florence that I had thought of her constantly since I had first set eyes on her at Reisenweber's. "Would you have supper with me when I return to New York next week?" I implored.

"I'm not sure, George. But you can call me. We live in the country and I don't go out very much." Not very encouraging, but a start.

We just made the station in time for the 2:00 A.M. train. Fay was furious and had boarded a few minutes before. We rushed for the platform but the gateman stopped us.

"Only those with tickets on the platform," he intoned in his most officious manner.

"But, my dear man," I said rather pompously, screwing my English monocle further into my eye, "this lady is my wife and I won't be seeing her for months." This line, read very sincerely, plus a large cigar, opened the gates for me. Then, a brief glance, a sweet, not too warm or passionate kiss, and I jumped off the train as it started to gather momentum.

All the following week I was in a lover's daze. I could think of nothing else but Florence. I consoled myself with the thought that after Johnstown I would be booked into the Bushwick Theater in Brooklyn. From there I could get a Long Island Railroad train and be at Florence's in half an hour—if I was invited.

In the midst of all this daydreaming, Rose and Curtis, my managers, wired me that my route had been changed. I would not come to the Bushwick for two more weeks. They had booked me in Petersburg, Newport News, and Richmond, Virginia. This was murder, not because it kept me away from Florence but because the hayseeds in those backwaters would not understand my *Hello, Mama* act or any of my gags. There was no way out.

I opened in Petersburg and flopped miserably. The headliner was J. C. Nugent, the father of playwright Elliott Nugent, who was trying out a new one-act play, *The Meal Hound*. Nugent fascinated me because he played a drunk in the sketch and in real life he had never taken a drink. The other performers told me that Nugent had watched me sympathetically in the first performance. When the show was over I went to his dressing room to talk to him.

"I'm sorry you saw me here today, Mr. Nugent. These people,

as I told my managers, don't understand my act. Do you have any suggestions?''

"Listen, son," he said in his best professorial voice, "don't ever blame this on me, but my advice is for you to get out of here quick. Get back into the big towns; that's where you belong.''

"You mean," I stammered, ". . . quit right after this three-day date?''

"No," replied Nugent rather firmly, "right now. These three days aren't going to get you anything, and it won't help the theater, either." I didn't feel that he had to add that last critique.

I was of mixed emotions.

"Gee, you're wonderful, Mr. Nugent. You don't know what this advice means to me. Not only about my act, but I'm stuck on a young lady in New York.''

"I knew that, too," he replied. "I could tell by the way you were singing.''

I was out of Petersburg within twenty-five minutes, leaving behind my music and a hurried note to the management that I had been taken terribly ill. The following night I was standing under a tree professing undying love for Florence. I was aided by all the elements of a warm Long Island evening.

For once I didn't resort to the "Indian Love Lyrics." They seemed very phony in this honest-to-goodness romance. Florence seemed to like me a lot.

"Now, go and make something of yourself," she said, very earnestly, "and we'll see what happens.''

The next morning, as are the ways of love, I was more full of ambition than I had ever been before, even more so than after the Marilyn Miller episode. The week after, I played the Bushwick and I went over very well. I followed at Keith's Boston and other big-time vaude houses until suddenly the New York actor's strike hit us all.

The casts of all Broadway shows were outside picketing, and there was talk that the musicians and stagehands would go out in sympathy and thereby close every legitimate theater in New York. I arrived in Gotham on a Monday morning, and Rose and Curtis sent me right over to Florenz Ziegfeld who had sent for me. He wanted to know if I could play Cantor's part in the Follies.

The news that the Great Ziegfeld had sent for me and commanded me to his august presence got around town very quickly. Rufus Le Maire—later a top executive at 20th Century-Fox—who was then acting for the Shuberts, also sent for me. Despite the fact that all was harmony between actors and managers, Ed Wynn, the star of *The Gaities*, had not returned to the cast. Henry Lewis had been hired in his stead but had been taken ill. Even though the Shuberts had never seen me perform, they would take a chance on me in the reopening of *The Gaities* at the Forty-fourth Street Theater. I gave J. J. Shubert a little idea of my stuff in the lobby of the theater. (I had previously told Ziegfeld that I would not cross picket lines.)

My act was to consist of talking to my mother and singing my own songs, "Oo, La La," and a new ballad I had composed, "Oh, How I Laugh When I Think How I Cried about You." (Can you imagine a contemporary band playing tunes like those today?)

I would do these numbers in two separate spots in the show and also play an opening scene until I could get up in the whole part. I was told by the wardrobe department to wear evening clothes during the opening scene, which took place at a garden party.

My entrance cue was, "Here comes Jack the rounder." Scintillating, eh? I then had to speak a few lines related to the plot itself, but with no laughs and a meaningless exit. I did not show myself until almost the last minute. Then I came down in my blue suit, a straw hat, and a cigar, just in time to hear my cue and walked on. One of the cast, as per script, said, "Tell us, Jack, what do you know about Mrs. Potter?"

I was supposed to reply, "She's dancing in the ballroom with young Hobbs, the architect. . . ."

I deliberately missed my cue for effect. "What?" I answered, and the actor repeated his line. "What do you know about Mrs. Potter?" He was becoming very exasperated not only because of my missed cue but because of my attire.

"Nothing. I'm from vaudeville, and I was only hired this morning. But I do know there's a good hotel near here if you want to take her there."

Then I suddenly went into a monologue; the stage manager and rest of the cast were apoplectic and the audience was rolling in the aisles. My monologue consisted mainly of my not knowing what the show was all about. My exit was to terrific, encore-type applause. I was in that same high key for the rest of the show, and the critic Burns Mantle said that ". . . Georgie Jessel was fearless in his Broadway debut."

The following day I was signed to a five-year contract by the Shuberts and the next morning I was married to Florence. In two days I learned the part in the play as it was originally written and cut out the ad-libbing. It did not go over with the audience. They expected, because of the word of mouth, my opening night facetiousness.

In the meantime, Florence was having trouble with her sister Fay about me. She was afraid that our marriage and my first big success would break up their act. I began to worry about my performance, and a few weeks later my contract was cancelled.

I was out of the show and Florence and I were not getting along very well.

5

Producing a Musical Play

I**N** the short time Florence and I had been married, I had made
rapid strides. The reason for my dismissal from *The Gaities* was
never known by anyone on Broadway. Broadwayites were only interested in opening nights. Second night hits or failures were unimportant. Keyed up by my first-night reception in a real show, I
worked feverishly and worried about my future. I had no desire to
return to vaudeville as a monologist. As an example, just before I
joined *The Gaities*, I had been booked for thirty weeks at good
money on the Keith Circuit and had cancelled the tour. That's how
sure I was of making it on Broadway.

Instead, I started work on a musical revue called *Georgie
Jessel's Troubles of 1919*, wherein I would play an East Side kid
who borrows his mother's widow's mite to start a Broadway show.
Then, after digging up the money and actors, there was to be a
strike. All this I had written in a broad, kidding manner except for
the scene between my mother and myself. For this scene I had written a song with Louis Silvers, "Mama's Baby Boy." With a brief
outline of the show in hand, I called on Al Lewis and Max Gordon
who were the most important vaudeville producers of the era.

44

Lewis was very enthusiastic about my idea but suggested I do it as a one-act play and perhaps later on it would materialize as a Broadway production. Such an act on the vaudeville circuit would command a lot of money and be a headline attraction. With Al Lewis I wrote the act, and it opened at the Palace in New York, where it was a big success.

As a result, *Troubles* was immediately booked for a tour from New York to the coast, and back again. Florence and I were still not getting along too well. It was really my fault that she was hurt because all I could talk to her about was what I heard Raymond Hitchcock talk about over lunch at Delmonico's that day and what I had said to various and sundry personalities along Broadway. I was so filled with my own self-importance, of being around big stars, that Florence's beautiful eyes did not seem as important as electric lights and pats on the back from my contemporaries. She continued to appear with her sister and we didn't meet again for six months or so.

During that time I had written *Troubles* into a full-blown musical play hoping for a Broadway production as Lewis had suggested earlier. But it did not come off. I had a great many promises, but after a month or two I gave up the idea. After the tour to the coast and back, I was out of work for quite some time. (It should be explained here that, in vaudeville in those days, "name" acts such as myself earned very good money. Anywhere from $500 to $1,500 per week. Consequently, if you were careful and didn't have too large an entourage, you could live well "between engagements." Money of that magnitude went a long way in those days.)

Florence returned to New York after her tour, but we weren't happy and decided to separate. Again, it was my fault. It was bad enough to have a husband who didn't pay much attention to you because he was working hard trying to make a hit, but to have a husband who was not attentive enough and out of work besides—well, you couldn't blame Florence. Besides, during the time she was away, she had become interested in the Christian Science religion then sweeping the country. And, like most people who are converted, she was converted well. The jokes and *schnapps* after midnight were out as far as she was concerned. That meant

I'd stay at the Friar's Club till the wee hours. I also decided to move out of our apartment.

For the first time in my life I carried a torch. The Friar's Club had a special floor set aside for men whose wives had left them or vice versa. After a couple of weeks of sitting up until all hours with four or five cronies discussing our marital woes, we all began trying to get our wives on the telephone. When I failed, I was terribly upset. The lawyer we had hired to draw up the separation papers had fallen in love with Florence, and so she insisted upon an immediate dissolution. I suspected this was the lawyer's idea more than hers. After planning seven or eight different ways of putting him out of commission, especially in the place where it counted, I calmed down and we were divorced. The lawyer, I might add, committed suicide a few years later.

It was about this time that the Shuberts advanced a new idea in show business in association with other theatrical managers throughout the country. There was to be a Shubert Vaudeville Circuit, which was not to be the customary variety show, but was to be a bill of five or six headline acts augmented by a chorus. Each of the acts were to participate in a musical revue for the second half of the show. In other words, a musical comedy in reach of the people in the sticks; but it was still to be called vaudeville. This was done so that the show could run twice daily and thus circumvent the new Equity rule—as a result of the strike—of eight performances a week.

This, I felt, was a chance for my brainchild *Troubles,* and I immediately made a deal. Unfortunately, I insisted they hire the Courtney Sisters as the featured players with me. They were not told it was my show until they had accepted all the conditions and the salary. It was then that I made my grand entrance into the Shubert office. Florence and I just shook hands.

But what a season that was.

Appearing in a play with my ex-wife, stuck on her again and each going to our separate rooms after the performance, we were both jealous as hell of each other and fighting like mad. Added to these emotional problems was the fact that the Shubert Vaudeville Circuit flopped.

My show and the Marx Brothers' and one or two others did

business, but the other twenty closed within two or three weeks. Consequently, there were no theaters for my attraction to play. But I wouldn't quit. I booked a series of one-night stands, taking the management on my shoulders and getting no salary for weeks. The other performers always got theirs, including Florence and Fay.

The climax to my venture into theatrical management came when we were due to play a one-nighter in Erie, Pennsylvania. Just as we arrived, the most violent storm of the decade hit the town, the electric service was shorted out, and the theater marquee was blown away.

I was left with a company of thirty on my hands and no money to pay them off. I eventually got hold of Lee Shubert and Eddie Cantor who wired the train fares. My misery on that train ride in that day coach from Erie is something I didn't forget for a hell of a long time. We boarded the train at 6:00 A.M. on a bitterly cold and damp morning. One of the local lads had sold me a bottle of "gin" for $1.50. I huddled in the back of the coach, opened the bottle, and found out it was the purest water I had ever tasted.

Before the journey was over, Florence came over to me and said she was sorry and hoped I would come out of it all right. We made a date for dinner the following week in New York, and I immediately went to work and wrote a sketch called *Mama in the Box*.

The subject of this skit was my taking my Yiddish mama to see a French play, explaining to her that it was a celebrated French drama and that she should try to understand it. If she couldn't, I would translate it for her in Yiddish. As part of the skit, I was also to translate the play into English for the audience.

Each time an actor spoke a line on the stage in French, I translated it for the audience and then to my mother in her native tongue. Mama, wearing a shawl around her and a funny hat on her head, meanwhile, sits there, eats an apple, and gets into running arguments with people in the audience. When one of the actors stopped the action of the play and excitedly said something to Mama in French, I translated it for her. She insulted him in Yiddish and he then returned the insult in the same jargon. The whole cast joined in and the curtain fell.

J. J. hired me immediately to do this sketch for the New Winter Garden Passing Show. I was back on Broadway again, not as a star, but with an act that was soon to be the laugh hit of Broadway. Just before rehearsals were due to start, I was having lunch with A. H. Woods, who at the time had six or seven successes playing throughout the country. "Come on, sweetheart," he said to me over brandy and cigars. "Catch the 20th Century with me tonight and spend a day in Chicago."

I jumped at the chance because I knew Florence and her sister were playing there. After Woods had completed his business at the theater, we both went backstage to visit Florence.

"Why don't you two get married again," said Woods, after Florence and I had embraced rather warmly. I think a tear or two was shed by both.

We were married that afternoon, but I had to take the late train back to New York to start rehearsals at the Winter Garden, and I didn't want anything to interfere with another major shot at Broadway.

That season was a very happy one indeed. Florence came back to New York and we rented a little house down the Island. All went well for the next six months, except that Florence's religious studies took her further and further away from show business. She and Fay gave up their act, and Fay blamed me for it. But it wasn't really my fault this time. My wife's eyes, which had once been so full of fire, had now taken on a soft, spiritual glow. And you cannot sing sexy (for those days) songs dressed in a slinky costume when you have just finished reading part of the New Testament. The voice—in Florence's case—was willing but the torso and psyche rebelled.

The Winter Garden show went on tour, and I went with it for a few weeks. I had a little money in my pocket and was itching with the producing bug. While playing in Boston, I received a phone call from Rufus Le Maire, by then an agent. He was in a jam and had contracted to produce a musical comedy that was being written by George S. Kaufman and Marc Connolly. Connolly and Kaufman were already highly successful on Broadway with *To the Ladies* and *Dulcy*, among others. The music and lyrics for Le Maire's production, *Helen of Troy, New York*, had already been written by

Bert Kalmar and Harry Ruby. Le Maire had given Connolly, Kaufman, et al. their first advance, but within a day or two he would have to come up with additional payments of $2,500 for Kaufman and Connolly, and $1,000 for Kalmar and Ruby. Not only didn't he have a dime, but he was being locked out of his office and his hotel room.

"But," he assured me over the telephone, "I don't want any money from you, Georgie. I'm going to get a big chunk from Nick the Greek and also $50,000 from two bootleggers I know who will come across as soon as they get a shipment ashore next week. So, all I need is time and I want you to send me a telegram.

"Don't even use your own name," went on Le Maire, not even pausing for breath or my reaction. "Any high-sounding name will do. And put in the wire that you are coming to New York to invest twenty or thirty thousand dollars in the show with me. This will tide me over and I'll never forget you."

To help out a friend, I sent him the following wire from Boston:

> Dear Rufus. After talking the matter over with my attorneys do not feel that I ought to put up all the money for "Troy" even though I have the highest respect for your authors and composers. But as I feel sure the show will be a success, I will invest $25,000. I will give you a check on my arrival next week.

I signed it with one of the fanciest names I could find. I happened to glance at the *Boston Globe* lying beside me and saw the Aga Khan's name mentioned as arriving in New York the following week. I thought it would be poetic justice to sign the telegram,

> Sincerely, Eugene A. Khan

I got the "Eugene" from another story on the same page about a crooked politician who had recently been sent to jail. Apropos, I felt.

I returned to New York the following week and immediately contacted Rufus. "The telegram did its work, Georgie. But Nick the Greek didn't lay off enough bets and he's broke. The bootleggers were hijacked. But I've got two other guys who'll come through in a week or two."

With a great flourish, Rufus whipped out a telegram almost identical to the one I had sent him, and I went for it, hook, line, and checkbook. I put up the dough he needed for the authors and lyricists and became a partner. I was in for the ten grand I had in the bank before I realized I was the only angel! And that, except for a few hundred dollars in walking-around money, was all I had.

In the meantime, we had hired a large chorus, some important actors and actresses, and I was worried. Rufus, who was young and daffy at the time, was confident that someone would throw the money needed for production over the transom. He was also very lavish with the salaries he was handing out. He was acting as their agent as well and getting ten percent. I wouldn't stand still for this until he declared me in.

We worked morning, noon, and night trying to get people interested. We set up several "auditions" to interest prospective investors, and Rufus would explain that a musical then on Broadway, *Sally, Irene, and Mary*, would make a million dollars. I would sing some of the lyrics while Kalmar and Ruby went through the scenes. We did this as often as a dozen times within twenty-four hours. Every possible source of money was thoroughly canvassed. Many times I went down to the fur district, visiting the offices of merchants I had met in the Clevelands, the Eries, and the Pittsburghs of the country. Naturally, it was to no avail; I couldn't raise a dime.

In the meantime, the show was in rehearsal at Bryant Hall at the rate of nine dollars per day. One afternoon after I had talked myself hoarse, pleading with a fellow who owned a chain of barber shops to put up some dough, I staggered into Bryant Hall in time to hear the owners of the joint tell Le Maire, "No more rehearsing until I get my money for the last two weeks."

Before this could spread to the cast, I shouted:

"Le Maire, the company is over-rehearsed. They're getting stale. No more rehearsals today!"

That night we brought my cousin Milford into the picture. He was younger than I, but we were always very close. He had been in the rag business and his company had gone under and I was teaching him the ins and outs of show business. Milford was particularly interested in the blonde part of show business and wore my very actory clothes. He also wore glasses and a brand-new mustache of which he was very proud. We arranged for him to walk in on us the following day at rehearsals and to say, loud enough for the owner's ears, that he and his father would put up all the money for the show. This would get us by for at least a few days. Milford felt this was not the right thing to do; but, with the promise of a jar of French mustache wax, he agreed and we were able to resume rehearsals.

Later that night there was a sad consultation at Billy La Hiff's, later known as Duffy's Tavern, where I had credit and where Le Maire was eating some gargantuan meals on my tab. Present at the meeting were Kalmar, Ruby, and Le Maire (who hadn't shaved for at least four days), myself, and Milford. I was ready to throw in the sponge and kiss my ten grand goodbye. I proposed that I would make the necessary speech to the actors to the effect that the play wasn't quite ready and that I had had words with Kaufman and Connolly, who didn't like me anyway, so it would be easy to get out of the whole thing without further disgrace.

Just then a telephone call came for Le Maire. One of his bootlegger friends wanted us to come immediately to a party in Yonkers. We rushed out of the tavern, hired a Packard on the cuff, and an hour later were in a cellar in Yonkers where there was quite a shindig going on. Le Maire's contact met us and we were introduced to a gentleman with the unlikely name of Butch Fink.

"Boys, do your stuff," said Butch, very much the host. "Sing the songs, tell the gags, and I think I'll get you the sugar from these hoods."

Ruby rushed to the broken-down piano, and Kalmar and I not only sang the songs from the show but also did everything we had ever done on the stage before. And when we ran out of material, Kalmar did a magic act. It was quite a party.

It turned out that our hosts, for want of a better term, had a shipment of whiskey they had made themselves out of town in a corner of the cellar and were busily making labels and bottling the stuff. I think they were using the name of Early Days for this batch. Early it was, having just come out of a mountain still. The label making went on all during our act, and the whole thing wound up in a fight. We were thrown out of the joint, got no money, and

Milford had to be taken to a doctor. He had been the first to sample
the new whiskey. Just how Le Maire handled the driver of the car
I'll never know. All I know is he laid low for a few days.

Six o'clock in the morning we wound up in the Automat. On
the table there was a copy of the *New York Times*, and in the theatrical section was an item that caught our eye.

> Wilmer and Vincent, the important theater owners from
> Pennsylvania, are interested in producing Broadway plays,
> especially dramas.

Le Maire, with his agent's *chutzpah*, suggested I contact them
immediately. I thought the idea was cuckoo to bring our plans to
them—they were undoubtedly interested in producing a one-set
drama or comedy and not a production that would cost upward of
sixty or seventy thousand dollars.

I agreed to see them, anyway, as soon as possible. I had something else up my sleeve, a little play that had been produced downtown in Greenwich Village. The play, *Dry Rot*, could be brought up
to Broadway for six or seven thousand dollars.

Wilmer and Vincent saw me that day, and, when I met these
fine, middle-aged showmen, I was positive that they wouldn't be interested in a girlie show. So I never mentioned it but tried to interest them in the production of *Dry Rot*.

"What is the story line, Mr. Jessel?" Mr. Vincent inquired
politely.

"It's about a British doctor living in the tropics and a native
girl called Tondeleyo. We can get the show on Broadway for six or
seven thousand," I explained, but it didn't interest them in the
slightest.

(Earl Carroll was later to bring *Dry Rot* to Broadway, change
the title to *White Cargo*, and make his first fortune.)

When I got up to leave their hotel room at the Astor, I was
given a fancy Cuban cigar. As I shook hands to leave, Wilmer
looked at me and said, "Is there anything around with music that
you know of?"

Within three hours they had heard the entire score and I had
read them the book of *Helen of Troy, New York*. The following
morning they put up $100,000.

During the out of town tryouts in Boston and Hartford, I became very friendly with George Kaufman, something I had been unable to accomplish until then. During rehearsals I had disagreed with George about a lot of the dialogue because I thought it was too satirical for a musical comedy, and too smart and sophisticated for the average New York theatergoer. In those days, shows were written and produced with the public in mind first, not the critics. Today it is the other way around and no play can survive bad reviews.

The *Helen of Troy* Kaufman and Connolly had written had kidding, satirical love scenes. The lovers never clinched, and the situations, though brilliantly written, were over everyone's head, including the cast.

Nevertheless, George and I made peace, and several years later he was to tell a close friend of mine, "I wish I were rich enough to hire Jessel to live with me all the time so I need never stop laughing."

Two weeks later we opened at the Selwyn Theater, and a very unpredictable thing happened. The comedienne of the show was Queenie Smith, a highly talented young lady who could do almost anything in the musical comedy line, as well as being an exquisite ballet dancer. She had gone over very well while we were trying out the show on the road, but after her ballet in New York she was an absolute sensation. Most of the critics, while fairly complimentary to the show as a whole, raved about Queenie, and rightly so. The opening night audience stood up and cheered. Some critic maintained, "Queenie Smith's performance alone was worth the evening. . . . " However, the cheering and applause were never repeated. Why, I'll never know. Perhaps the fire that performers have on opening night burns out by the time the second performance rolls around. Anyway, because the book was a bit too satirical, as I had warned, and the lyrics much too Rodgers and Hartsy for the times, the show closed after a few months. I got back most of my ten thou, but the show lost a great deal of money.

Only Rufus Le Maire got out from under. He had an uncanny knack of being closer to the guy on the street than any of us, and he knew we didn't have a hit. He sold his interest right after opening night—and that is how I got most of my money back—it was a loan to him, not an investment in the show.

In the meantime, seeing the writing on the wall, I had written a new vaudeville act, *Go Back Home*, in which I did a monologue. Two little girls were to come up on the stage and interrupt it with, "Please, Mr. Jessel, we want you to put us on the stage."

Then, in a nostalgic manner, I told them they were in the springtime of their youth and should not spend those golden hours in a dressing room. I finished the speech with: "I've been on the stage all my life. When I first started, I had only two dollars in my pocket, and look at me now. I owe thousands."

Then I would sing, "Little Rover, Think It Over and Don't Forget to Come Back Home." (Gad!)

I opened the act at the Orpheum Theater in Chicago and was a big hit. I was particularly pleased the next day to read the *Chicago American*, which gave me a series of wonderful compliments. I was to the show, the critic said, "what fine brandy, coffee and a cigar are to a good dinner."

I asked the manager to arrange a meeting for me with the critic. When I met him, he acted as though he had never seen me in his life. I found out later that he had been on a two-day drunk, had not been at the theater at all, and a friend of his, an advance publicity man, had written the copy for him. This young friend was Jed Harris, later one of the great show business minds of the theater and with whom I was later to be associated.

The following week I played Milwaukee. One night I threw a party in my hotel suite with good Rhine wine and a tray of cold cuts from the local deli. I always carried a phonograph with me, and I put on one opera record after another. I also carried some two hundred or more records with me, and I needed a moving van to get to the railroad stations at every stop. Among the vaudeville performers in my room that night was an extremely attractive girl to whom I was soon whispering part of the "Indian Love Lyrics."

This was followed by a very passionate "let's-go-to-bed" embrace, and almost on cue Florence walked in the door deciding to pay me a surprise visit.

The party ended rather abruptly, and I went on to play my act the following matinee with a very neat bandage wrapped around my skull. Florence had crowned me with a stack of Caruso records.

(Right) "The Immortal Bard," an oil portrait by famous artist John Decker, pal and confidant of Barrymore, me, and Hollywood in general. (Below) The Gus Edwards *Song Revue,* Gus's most successful show and my first "break," until the Gerry Society got into the act. I'm second from the left at the bottom, Gus Edwards at the piano, and Walter Winchell is above Gus's head. Georgie Price is at the far right of the photo. Lila Lee, then known as "Cuddles," is second from the right on top of the piano.

Me with Eddie Cantor in *Kid Kabaret* in San Francisco. I'm in my "Chaplin imitation" hairdo. (1912)

(Top left) As *The Jazz Singer*, perhaps one of my most famous roles on the Broadway stage. (Photo by White Studio) (Top right) From the famous last act of *The Jazz Singer*. (Bottom left) With Norma Talmadge in a pose for my *Hello, Mama* telephone act. (1932) (Associated Press Photo) (Bottom right) With Irving Berlin in New York. (1959)

(Top left) With "The Great Profile," John Barrymore. (Top right) With June Haver, a girl I really discovered, on the set of my picture *I Wonder Who's Kissing Her Now* at 20th Century-Fox. (1946) (Bottom left) With Crosby at a Pirates game in Pittsburgh in 1947. Crosby, together with Bob Hope, owned a piece of the team. (Bottom right) With Jack Benny at a Friars Club Frolic in New York in 1948. Jack was "dressing" as Gracie Allen to act as a foil for George Burns. Since women were not allowed at these affairs, Jack agreed to "substitute" for Gracie.

(Above) With comedian Harry Hirschfield, Milton Berle, and Eddie Cantor at a testimonial dinner for me in New York. (1952) (Below, left to right) Ernest Hemingway, Mrs. Hemingway, Mrs. Leland Hayward, Spencer Tracy, myself, and agent Leland Hayward at the Stork Club around 1957.

(Top left) With Shirley Temple at the Hollywood Press Photographers Costume Ball.
won the prize as General Grant. (Top right) With Abigail Adams and Ann Blythe at a Fox
luncheon for theater owners. I addressed the exhibitors as "the oldest living theater
owner." (Photo: Charles Rhodes) (Bottom left) With Walter Winchell in one of our friend
lier moments in 1958. (Bottom right) With old pal Rudy Vallee at a buffet supper in Holly
wood following an opening. It was free (including the parking), so Rudy came.

(Above) On the Merv Griffin Show, the only talk show I am allowed on because of my outspoken views on Madison Avenue and the liberal press. (1972) (Below) At an opening in Santa Barbara in 1973. My manager/publicist Stanley Cowan is on the left.

With Stanley Cowan in 1975.

6

The Jazz Singer *and Norma Talmadge*

IN the summer of 1925 I was hired to appear in an ultra-smart nightclub, the Café de Paris on Fifty-fourth Street. This was to be a big show with Isham Jones and his band from Chicago, myself as emcee, and, as the featured attraction, the Ziegfeld song star Bea Palmer.

Bea was very attractive and had a new and effective style of singing. But she was a bitch, to put it mildly. She and her accompanist were also married and fought all the time. A more temperamental singer had never walked down Broadway before. Bea never, for instance, showed up for rehearsals because her pianist-husband ran through her numbers for timing purposes; but we were not worried. We felt she was a professional and would show up by showtime. By midnight, when the show was scheduled to begin, Bea had still not made an appearance. The band played, I did everything I had ever done in show business, and I kept reminding the audience that at almost any moment they would soon be entertained by "the lady Al Jolson."

At one-thirty I was still stalling for time, and I had to ask for help from the audience. I called on Nora Bayes to come up and sing

55

"Shine on, Harvest Moon," Eddie Cantor did fifteen or twenty minutes, others took bows, and then there was no one left to call upon.

Sitting in a corner was a young, good-looking fellow whom I only knew by name. He had been a songwriter, lawyer, then an assemblyman and New York state senator. At the moment, he was acting in some official capacity for a bottled water company and presumably was in the café on his expense account. I had heard him speak at a dinner and felt sure he could hold an audience —even a noisy nightclub crowd. However, following a lot of stars, you sure as hell couldn't get up and say, "Now, ladies and gentlemen, an ex-senator, now in the mineral water business, will say a few words . . .."

I thought on my feet and asked Isham to play a loud fanfare and end it with a cymbal crash from the drummer. Then, with great dignity, I blurted out: "Ladies and gentlemen, as you know, you will soon be entertained by that great artist, Miss Bea Palmer, if she shows up. However, my young, but tired and watery eyes have found in this rendezvous of gaiety a young man who may be the next mayor of this great city of New York, the former senator, James J. Walker."

Walker, whom I had never met personally, walked toward me on the dance floor and whispered, "Where the hell did you get that idea from, young fella?" He then turned to the audience and held them fascinated for a full half hour about what he would do for the city if he were elected mayor. In the meantime, Bea Palmer arrived.

About ten days later, Walker telephoned me at the St. Regis.

"Son, you're either a fortune teller or else you've got a pipeline to Tammany Hall. I've just received the nomination to run for mayor."

During Jimmy's successful campaign, I made fifty speeches throughout Brooklyn and the Bronx. Jimmy Walker and I became the very closest of friends. All the way up, all the way down, and, thank God, all the way up again. When most New Yorkers felt Jimmy had fallen from grace, I knew it wasn't so. When politics in New York needed a fall guy—and it does every decade or so, even today—Jim was picked. I testified to his goodness at every public function I attended. But the just need no defense, and there was, toward the end of his life, no more popular man in New York. I have always been grateful for his friendship and counsel.

Later on that summer, Lewis and Gordon sent for me. They had now branched out into more than just vaudeville producers and had an interest in several Broadway plays in association with Sam H. Harris. Lewis had on his desk a manuscript called "The Day of Atonement." This was a dramatization by a very youthful author of his story printed in *Everybody's* magazine. The script, which was much too short for a play, had already been on the desks of several managers who had liked the idea, but all were certain that it needed a great deal of work. Like most young authors, Sampson Raphaelson didn't want his brainchild touched. Al Lewis, however, had a way with authors, and he convinced Sampson that, since the leading role in the play was that of an entertainer, whoever played the part would take a great many liberties. Lewis thought I was the guy for it. I had never appeared in a legitimate play before. But, from the pathos in my *Troubles* act, and the phone calls to my mother, Lewis was confident that my appearance in a serious play would be the making of me as a top-flight performer.

The author, Lewis, and I set to work, and six weeks later "The Day of Atonement" opened in Stamford, Connecticut. It was a great success under the new title *The Jazz Singer*, and it came to New York and the Fulton Theater three weeks later.

The Jazz Singer, for those of you who don't know the story, is the tale of a boy who runs away from a religious household. The boy, who comes from a family whose father's fathers were all synagogue cantors, becomes a successful blackfaced jazz singer. Yet, on the eve of his opportunity to become a great star, he returns to his dying father's bedside. He takes the old man's place in the synagogue with the solemn vow never to leave again. The play had a great audience appeal, but the critics damned it after its opening night.

One magazine critic, Alan Dale, who is now dead but who never squared himself with me, said: "Among the openings last week was 'The Jazz Singer' with the vaudeville actor, George Jessel. It is needless for me to write about this play since this magazine will not be out for two weeks and, in all probability 'The Jazz Singer' will be closed by that time."

I was still playing the role a year and a half later.

The other critics, while panning the play, were particularly kind to me personally, especially George Jean Nathan. Within three weeks, in spite of the reviews, we were playing to standing room only. *The Jazz Singer* was destined to turn the amusement world on its tail since it was one of the principal reasons for the beginning of sound films.

However, the tragic story of this young Jewish boy, his simple mother, her neighbors, and his father who believed that songs should only be chanted in praise of God, had a universal appeal. I played one performance for a thousand priests; I acted scenes from the play in churches and temples across the United States. It became a subject for sermons in every city we played.

The play was at the end of its first year's run in New York. Many people came to see the show three and four times. Sam Bernard, the great Broadway comedian, came every night for four months, sitting in my dressing room and then going out front or standing in the wings to watch the last act in which my father dies and I sing the sacred "Kol Nidre" in the synagogue. Irving Berlin and Ellen Mackay attended six times. David Belasco wrote me a note to the effect that he was sorry he had waited such a long time to see the play. Even though he had heard so much about it, he had been thrilled beyond his expectations. The day after I received this note, I rushed to his office.

"May I please see him for a moment?" I asked the receptionist.

I was ushered into his office immediately, and a soft light over his desk was aimed directly at Belasco's head.

"Mr. Belasco," I started, "I am deeply honored to have received your letter. Would it be impertinent of me if I used it as an ad for my play?"

I stepped back a few paces not knowing what the reaction from the Great Belasco would be after asking to quote a personal note in anything so crass as an advertisement. He smiled, ran his fingers through his hair, and looked me in the eye.

"I will be hurt if you don't, young man!"

I used to hold out four "house seats" every night in my name at the box office of the Cort Theater where the show had moved. If any of my friends called me at the last minute, they could have them. If no one called, I would notify the box office by eight o'clock to sell the seats. Very often, I would call the box office before the curtain to inquire as to who had purchased the seats. If they were people of any prominence, my part was so elastic I might incorporate their names somewhere in one of the gayer scenes of the piece. One night I was told that Norma Talmadge and a party of three had my seats. I had never seen Norma Talmadge before but had always been a great admirer of hers as a screen actress. Right after I walked on stage, I quickly spotted her. I watched her throughout the entire performance.

Miss Talmadge, who was a Catholic, and whose background was so far removed from the locale of the play, the old East Side of New York, was profoundly moved by the story. As I made my curtain speech, she stood and applauded. The following night she came again and the next night after that.

My very dear friend, Sam Harris, who owned fifty percent of the show, called me up and invited Florence and me to come to his home in Great Neck for Sunday dinner. This was early in April and the day was sunny but cold. The other guests at dinner were Norma and her husband, Joseph Schenck, Mr. and Mrs. Arthur Hammerstein, and Alexander Woollcot. I gazed out of the window at Long Island Sound. "I think I'll take a swim," I announced.

I was warned I'd freeze to death but, show-off that I was, I got into a pair of swim trunks proffered by the butler and a few minutes later dived off Harris's dock. It was like ice, but I was determined to go through with it. When I came back, Norma Talmadge was waiting for me with blankets and a shot of whiskey.

"This is awfully nice of you," I stammered through chattering teeth.

"I had the strangest feeling when you were out there. Maybe I'll tell you about it sometime. . . ." She said this with a very faraway look in her eyes as we walked back up to the house, me draped in a blanket and still shivering, Norma, looking very sedate and ethereal.

Later at dinner, and because of the company, the picture possibilities of *The Jazz Singer* were discussed at length. Despite the fact that it was a great Broadway smash, there had been no offers for it. Because of the subject matter, the great moguls of Hollywood did not feel that the general public would be interested. Joe Schenck, however, was not quite sure that he agreed with me, but I felt positive that if you see a sympathetic human being in distress, whether on stage or screen, you don't say to yourself, "I won't feel sorry for him because his religion is different than mine."

Norma, Joe, Florence, and I drove back to town later that night and parted with a very perfunctory goodbye, and "if you ever come to the coast, Mr. Jessel, you must dine with us."

My meeting with Norma Talmadge, at least the first one, was over. But I never forgot the words she had said to me earlier when I came out of the water. All through the night I was tormented by the thought that this beautiful woman was keeping some secret from me. Perhaps it was destined that some day we might be together. Maybe she was thinking of some picture in which I might play a part. What was it?

From then on, every girl I met only suffered by comparison. I was also still married to Florence. But for a while I succeeded in forgetting all about Norma. But in those days I never slept very much and found myself in the speakeasies later and later, or earlier and earlier, every morning, usually winding up in the company of playwright Samuel Shipman.

One night, Shippy called me at the theater just as I was changing for another foray on the town. He said there was a great new speak called the Helen Morgan Club that had opened a night or two earlier. (Speakeasies were illegal and the only "advertising" was word of mouth. It usually took a week or two for the word to spread.)

Helen Morgan had arrived in New York from Chicago only a few months before and had been causing a sensation with her singing. I had never heard her, although I had heard about her. Shippy and I met, and just as we arrived, the club quieted as though it had been hushed by a miracle and Helen started to sing. Her large chiffon handkerchief was wound around her hands as she let loose as only she could, and she held the audience enthralled. No matter how gay the lyrics, she sang them with a tear.

She closed her show with a new song she was to make famous in *Show Boat*—"Can't Help Lovin' That Man o' Mine." Shippy knew Helen and introduced us.

"You have a wonderful talent, Miss Morgan. I don't recall such a style as yours in all my years in the business. You sing your songs as if Whistler had painted them." (This was my new version of the "Indian Love Lyrics!")

Apparently, Helen had never before been spoken to like this, and she made a good audience listening to me for quite a while. After the club closed, she invited a few friends to her private bar upstairs where she sang until morning. In high hat, frock coat, and spats, I listened to her until 8:00 A.M.

Helen and I were as gay as birds and went out for breakfast. I began to call for her nearly every morning around four or five o'clock. We certainly didn't sit and chat, either. Florence was away and I had moved into the Warwick Hotel where Helen had a suite. I hated to get up to go home.

One day over lunch at Delmonico's, I met a motion picture crowd in from the coast, several of whom I had known from one of my sojourns in Never-Never Land. With them was Priscilla Dean, then Universal's top silent star, in New York for personal appearances. After dining together after the show, I took Priscilla to meet Helen and hear her sing. After introducing her, I told Helen I would be back at the hotel as soon as I had escorted Miss Dean to the Waldorf. I returned to the Warwick about 5:00 A.M. As I walked through the lobby, the telephone operator advised me that Helen had returned to her rooms. I should have given her a chance to finish what she wanted to tell me.

I rushed down the hall to Helen's room, used my key to open the door, and found her in bed with Mark Hellinger, the columnist and show business reporter, later a brilliant film producer. (Actually, it was Mark who started filling stars full of martinis before interviewing them. "Helps loosen the tongue so I can get the truth," he once told me.)

After viewing Helen *in flagrante delicto,* or whatever the expression is, I said nothing, too embarrassed to find words to fit the occasion. But not Helen; she raised hell with *me!* Offense to her was the best defense.

"How *dare* you bring another woman to my club," she stormed, not even bothering to cover her boobs, as most women do under those circumstances.

"Helen, my dear," I replied, trying to be dignified under rather difficult circumstances, "you know who that lady is, and she knows how fond I am of you. That was just a little courtesy. Anyway, what right have you to squawk at my indiscretion? *You're* in *bed* with another man!" All of this was said in what I felt was the correct tone of righteous indignation. Mark was laughing like hell.

"Don't change the subject," she screamed.

And that was the end of that. I left in a huff and made up my mind that there was only one woman for me and there never could be anyone else. But it would do me no good, for she was rich, world famous, far away, and married. It served me right, anyway.

Who goes swimming in Long Island Sound in April?

Only seals wearing mink.

7

Hollywood Was Never Very Kind

My association with motion pictures really dates back to 1911. In that year, Thomas A. Edison had an idea for sound films, and the first experiments were tried at an uptown studio. Gus Edwards arranged to have Cantor, Truly Shattuck, a well-known *prima donna* of the period, and me make the original tests. These were tried in a theater but were way out of sync, and that was the end of that. Nevertheless, we picked up a few bucks, which always came in handy.

Now and then, during the lay-off season, I used to do bits in the few pictures that were being made in New York and pick up maybe ten or fifteen dollars a day. I appeared in one called *The Other Man's Wife* in 1917 produced by Warner Brothers in which nearly the entire Warner family appeared. The Warners and I were very close friends, and I was particularly close to Sam. Like the Sam of the Shubert family, he had the warmest personality of all of the Warner brothers.

Sam came to my dressing room a few nights after the Helen Morgan fiasco with an offer from the then up and coming Warner Brothers to make a picture called *Private Izzy Murphy*. Jack was

63

preparing the story on the coast and was very enthusiastic about it. A young man who had just been brought into the company to assume a post as production assistant to Jack was also very high on the film's potential. His name was Darryl F. Zanuck and many, many years later I was to spend almost eleven very happy years producing musicals for this genius of the motion picture industry. But that comes later.

Zanuck was due in New York and the Warners said he would talk to me about the project. My first thought, however, was to do *The Jazz Singer* as a film. H. M. Warner, who ran the company from a business standpoint, was on the fence about purchasing the film rights.

"If we do well with *Izzy Murphy*," he told me, "we might buy it. I don't think it will make any money, but it would be a good picture to do for the sake of religious tolerance, if nothing else."

Sam Warner, who was with us, told H. M. and myself, "If this Vitaphone thing we're playing with [sound on disc] goes through by next year, we could make *The Jazz Singer* with sound and then you could sing the songs."

This was a great idea and I immediately began talking screenplay, or scenario as it was called in those days. "But," piped up H. M., "who knows what is going to happen with these crazy phonograph records? We are up to our necks in it now."

To prove my point, however, I went to the Vitaphone recording studio in the Manhattan Opera House a week later and made the first monologue ever done for movies, a two-reeler.

Called *Talking to Mother*, it was played at the original opening of the first Vitaphone show in New York and was a great success, at least from a novelty standpoint. For a demonstration of Vitaphone, I did two more two-reelers. As a result of their success, H. M. decided to try and go ahead and make a deal for *The Jazz Singer* even though the Warners were pretty well strapped financially. I helped them out through my influence with Harris, Lewis, and Gordon, and they were able to make the purchase for fifty-odd thousand dollars payable, if you please, with notes dated as far as a year and a half in the future. If it had not been for me, the Warner brothers would not have been able to pull off such a no-cash deal. Harris, Lewis, and Gordon were only too pleased, actually, to make a deal for *The Jazz Singer*, but they would have liked to have had some cash "up front."

Two months later my entire entourage, including Florence and Milford, left for California. We looked like a traveling circus with trunks upon trunks, my phonograph and boxes of records, and Florence's wardrobe trunks. But in those days you could take practically all the luggage you wanted by train. Jimmy Walker came to see us off, and we were surrounded by quite a rubbernecking crowd who recognized Jimmy, myself, and then Ted Healey, the comic.

On our arrival late in June, I rented a bungalow at the Beverly Hills Hotel, which pleased Florence very much. She could sit and concentrate on the Scriptures to her heart's content as it was similar to our own cottage on Long Island.

The following day I made the trek to the Warner Brothers studio on Sunset Boulevard in Hollywood. *Private Izzy Murphy* was in the hands of a former Keystone Kop director, Herm Lerner, whom everyone called "Pathe." He had never seen me on a stage and had no idea what I did or how I did it. For four or five hours he kept me sitting around the stage while he played mechanical-device scenes with several other comics. The first day I worked, we started at 5:00 A.M. and he had me do a scene over and over again insisting that I was not "sparkling enough." It was obvious to me that he resented any stage actor when he had been used to dealing with people who had started and spent their careers in front of a camera instead of an audience.

"I didn't know I had been hired as a bottle of Canada Dry," I cracked.

A few minutes later, Pathe became very ill and an assistant director, Lloyd Bacon, was given the job of finishing the film. Lloyd and I were later to make many successful films together at 20th Century-Fox. I always remembered him because, as the son of the famous actor Frank Bacon, he inherited a great deal of his father's feeling for the theater and handled stage actors accordingly—not like cattle as Pathe did.

Lloyd immediately removed all Pathe's slapstick and played

the film for its melodramatic value. After the second week and seeing what Lloyd could do, Zanuck recommended that Warner
Brothers give him a long-term contract.

To undo what had been done in the film necessitated working
forty-eight hours at a stretch. The scenes that we were making were
battle scenes and they were done very realistically. I was in a
"trench" for three hours and was stepped on and stepped over by
the hobnailed boots of German-soldier extras for what seemed like
thirty-three hours. If it hadn't been for many bottles of Coca-Cola
spiked with gin I would never have made it. I bless the prop man to
this day.

When I returned to the Beverly Hills Hotel each night, Florence greeted me in her ethereal white gown surrounded by as many
bibles and books on the Scripture as she could find. The local
Christian Science Church also saw that she was well supplied. It
made me feel as though I didn't belong. In fact, she told me very
plainly one night that Error should be destroyed and that I was
Error. The next day I moved into an apartment with Bob Benchley, Donald Ogden Stewart, and Herman Mankiewicz. Florence returned to New York, and again we were separated for quite a
while.

I left for New York, still in my makeup, at the completion of
the film. We finished the final scenes less than an hour before the
train was due to leave Pasadena. All in all it had been fun.

I went on tour again with *The Jazz Singer* and a few months
later *Izzy Murphy* was released—and very successfully. The Vitaphone Company was doing very well, and it was agreed with the
Warner frères that I would do the film version with sound the following summer.

When the original contract was signed, there had been no deal
for sound pictures. I pleaded with H. M. that the least they, the
Warners, could do, was to change my contract or give me a bonus.
H. M. was having a tough time with the financing of the company;
he was a very ambitious man and perhaps at that time he was stepping out in too many directions. It took him seven months to pay
me the $2,500 each for the three shorts I made for the Vitaphone
Company, giving me three checks for $2,500 each.

The record of the company, of course, shows that H. M. knew

what he was doing, but as far as I was concerned, I wanted a new deal. He talked about "taking care" of me if the picture was a success. I did not feel that was enough. We had a very heated argument, and he closed it by saying that I would do no pictures for the Warner brothers or anyone else in Hollywood if I persisted. He took an oath on his family's life on this statement. Both Sam and Jack, however, felt this could be patched up, and at the designated time, I went to Hollywood to start work. My first look at the scenario threw me into a state of shock, almost apoplexy.

Instead of the boy leaving the theater and following the traditions of his father by singing in the synagogue, as in the play, the scenario had him return to the Winter Garden as a blackfaced comedian with his mother applauding wildly from a box seat. I raised hell. Money or no money, I would not do this version. I had a feeling Jolson had a hand in all this because he had told many people he wanted to do the film version.

Apart from the script, I was still insisting on being paid "up front" and in cash. I had been getting $2,500 for each picture from the Warners. For the longer *Jazz Singer*, I asked for $5,000 and would have done it for that. But the same day I read the script all three checks the Warners had given me in New York for the three two-reelers bounced and caught up with me on the coast. This, I told Jack, was the reason I wanted my salary for *The Jazz Singer* up front. In addition, I wanted the three checks for $7,500 (total) made good before I started work.

I then went down to the Biltmore Theater where Al Jolson was headlining for a week. I told him my problems with the brothers Warner. He told me I was perfectly right, but in his usual offhanded, couldn't-care-less attitude. We had supper together in the Biltmore Rendezvous, and Jolie suggested I stay in his suite at the hotel because it was late. When I awoke the next morning, Al was dressing. "Go back to sleep, Georgie, I'm going to play golf. I'll see ya later. . . ."

The following morning I picked up the *Los Angeles Times* and read that Jolie had signed a contract the previous day—the day he was supposed to be playing golf—to star in *The Jazz Singer*. It threw me for a loop, and I couldn't even get Jack or Darryl on the telephone. I set out to find the reason why this had happened.

It turned out to be a matter of finances. For two weeks prior to his Biltmore date, Morris Safier, a Warner relative, had been negotiating with Jolie in Denver to see if he could put up the money to help finance the film. Jolie, at the time, was worth at least $5 million; he could well afford it. The Warners obviously knew I wouldn't (and couldn't) put up a dime. On top of that I wanted those bum checks made good, plus the $5,000.

Jolie agreed to put up $180,000 cash to get the film off the ground. To partly secure the notes, the Warners also gave Jolie some Goldman-Sachs stock then worth $30 a share. They told Jolie they had an "inside tip" that it would double or triple in a few months. It did; it rose to $140 and then plummeted a few weeks after Jolie sold out. I bought at $40 and sold out at 40¢.

Because of the box office success of *The Jazz Singer* and the stock sale, Jolie made another fortune off the film, in a role I created on Broadway. I had had my heart set on doing the film version. The only reason I can figure that the Warners had me come to Hollywood at all was to keep me out of New York when the checks bounced.

Al and I didn't speak for a year. When we did meet again, Jolie had the gall to tell me he "had to play the role because it is the story of my life!"

That was about as true as Jolie being at the crossing of the Delaware. Jack and I remained friendly over the years; that is, as friendly as anyone could be with him.

Nevertheless, I was still in Hollywood and the Warners had to make a picture with me to fulfill my contract. I was told by those in the know that the two they had scheduled for me were not going to be much good, and if I were smart, which I was not to the ways of Hollywood, I should make a contract adjustment and quit. I needed the money—particularly in view of the bum checks—and I made two more silents. When completed, they were finally shown at a few penitentiaries and a comfort station or two.

One of these was called *Sailor Murphy* and the director was again my nemesis, Pathe. He had me playing the part of a lunatic (which I was rapidly becoming) who believed he was an admiral. In one scene I had to be thrown into the Pacific Ocean off San Pedro in full admiral's uniform, sword and all, to be picked up by a nearby boat. Obviously trying to get back at me for *Izzy Murphy*, Pathe made me do that damn scene six times before he was satisfied. I was nearly drowned on the sixth take. I ended up the day by throwing every missile at Pathe I could find that wasn't secured to the dock.

During my stay in Hollywood, I saw Norma only once. She and Joe Schenck were separated by this time, and the talk was that Norma and her current leading man, Gilbert Roland, were madly in love with each other. I left for New York beaten and bewildered to resume my third season on tour with *The Jazz Singer*.

During the show's run at the City Theater on Fourteenth Street, a most interesting young lady came to town accompanied by her mother. She was Lita Grey Chaplin, very young, very beautiful—as were all of Charlie's wives—and she had just been divorced from the greatest screen comic of them all—past, present, and probably future.

This turned out to be Lita's first visit to New York, and she had been told by friends to be sure to see the show and meet Georgie Jessel. After attending one matinee she was brought backstage and introduced to me. I suggested supper that evening, with her mother, at the 400 Club, at the time the smartest of the New York speaks.

After spending several evenings together after the show, Lita and I agreed to continue our liaison while I was in Washington, D.C., the following week. We liked each other and she reminded me a great deal of Florence—the way she used to be before she "got religion." We were still married, mind you, but we both accepted the fact that we had to live separate and different lives.

The day Lita arrived in the capital, Mrs. Calvin Coolidge came to see the show. The following day, George Clark, the president's secretary, sent me an invitation to have tea with the president. The invitation, of course, included "Mrs. Jessel." I decided to take Lita, as Florence was reading the scriptures and the *Christian Science Monitor* in New York. Lita had received a lot of publicity over her divorce from Charlie and had been on the front pages of most of the newspapers and fan magazines for several weeks. Her face, by now, was as well known as Chaplin's.

Lita was dressed like a typical Hollywood film star, circa 1920, a long cigarette holder, heavy makeup, a boa, and flowing robes. When I introduced her to Coolidge, I thought he would faint. After all, I was a married man and Hollywood and show business personalities were not at the time as *persona grata* in the Oval Office as they have been the past two decades. Luckily, to save me embarrassment, the president made no reference to the real "Mrs. Jessel," just shook Lita's hand without a word.

But as Coolidge shook my hand, he said the very thing I expected to hear, yet hoped I wouldn't. "How are you, young man, and how is my friend Al Jolson?"

To be polite in the presence of the president of the United States, we chatted a little about Jolie and Will Rogers as well. Just as I was warming up to this man, who was considered very cold by most people, Clark stepped into the office and excused himself to the president.

"Mr. President, there is a man outside who voted for Mr. Lincoln and he wants to shake your hand. He's a very old man, so, do you think you could see him for a moment?"

Coolidge replied with a very quick yes, and a bearded and gaunt old man was ushered in. He took Coolidge's hand and shook it warmly. With emotion, he said, "By God, Mr. Coolidge, I voted for Abe Lincoln and I hope to live to vote for you again."

The president dropped the man's hand like a hot potato and dismissed him as quickly as he could. Then he turned back to me. "That's the trouble with this world. When you don't want something, everybody wants to give it to you."

A few days later Coolidge made his famous pronouncement: "I do not choose to run again."

Lita and her mother went back to the coast, but we made a date a long way off. She was going to Europe late in March and had passage arranged that would bring her to London on the first of April. I quickly checked the sailing schedules and promised to meet her at the Savoy Hotel on the night of April 3, my birthday.

A week or two after the show closed in Washington, the sound version of *The Jazz Singer* was sweeping the country, and I was swept out of business. I couldn't compete with a picture theater across the street showing the first great sound picture in the world, no matter how crude, and everything else the picture palaces of the day gave you for fifty cents, when we were charging three dollars a seat. The curtain fell on my most successful show, and I made a curtain speech to a very small audience berating what had been done to me by Jolie and Hollywood in particular.

I should have waited; there was more to come in my adventures with Hollywood. I was engaged by other companies who were entirely insensitive to what I had to offer as an actor and showman. They gave me jobs because I might be useful as an after-dinner speaker, or at making speeches at previews of big pictures. Universal had me under contract for a year. For the first four months, no one ever called me except to ask for a tip on the horses. It was known that Al Vanderbilt and I palled around while he was in Hollywood, and he generally had something going at one of the tracks.

Another time I had an idea for a picture I wanted to write and produce to star Fannie Brice and Beatrice Lillie. I had contacted both of them, and they were enthusiastic about the idea.

To show the mentality and provincialism of the picture people of those days, I went to the front office and discussed it with Charles Rogers, one of the chief executives of the company. "And what do they do, this Brice and Lillie?"

"They jump through hoops, you dumb son of a bitch."

Needless to say I was out on my ass the next day.

At another studio, for Sol Lesser Productions, I prepared a picture for production written by Joseph Fields and Jerry Chordorov who were later to write the comedy hits *My Sister Eileen* and *Junior Miss*. Their screenplay, which I wanted to do, was full of the same brilliant writing that was to be found later in their two stage hits. Lesser told me to fire them, that they were awful. Then I was fired.

At another studio, a few years later, I was brought in to create a story for a little boy called Bobby Breen who had appeared on Eddie Cantor's radio show. After completing work on the story, in which I was to have a financial interest as well as a part in the film, I was told by the director, Ray Chandler: "The kid is no good. Your title is no good, and we are calling the whole thing off. Here's a grand for your trouble. Just sign these papers for the file. They don't mean anything."

As soon as I had signed the papers, the Bobby Breen picture was made with my title and the major portion of my ideas—and the film made a fortune.

8

One Success and Three Failures

In 1928, Al Lewis and I were in Hollywood. I was there (again) to make two pictures in four weeks for a newly organized independent company, Tiffany-Stahl. These were to be very inexpensive silent films. The director's usual admonition at the close of day was, "Remember, folks, we start shooting tomorrow at 8:30 whether the actors are here or not."

It was early summer, and I thought while I was out there, I might hit upon an idea for a new stage play. Lewis and I had witnessed a performance at the Writers Club that included a one-act play by Commodore Richard Shayer called *Private Jones*. The story line concerned a boy in the army who meets another soldier, a boy whom he has hated for many years. Under a gas attack they both die together. One of these parts was played beautifully by Owen Moore, the first husband of Mary Pickford. Lewis and I bought the rights to this one-act play for practically nothing with the idea in mind that we would write two acts showing the reason why the boy hated his fellow soldier. Then we would add the last act we had just purchased.

Then the question arose: Who would I get to collaborate with

72

me? For many years I had been a great admirer of Ben Hecht. Al was getting ready to produce another Hecht play and offered to go to New York immediately to arrange a deal so that I could start working with Ben as soon as my picture was finished.

The rage of Hollywood at the time was Lupe Velez. The petite and fiery Mexican actress had just made her initial appearance on the screen with Douglas Fairbanks in *The Gaucho*. It was being gossiped around that Al Jolson was crazy about Lupe and had been dating her whenever he was in town. I decided to steal a march on Jolie as I had a crush on Lupe myself.

Lupe was appearing at a local theater in a Mexican play for the Los Angeles Mexican population. A mutual friend took me backstage to her dressing room. Standing outside her door, I brought back my Jolson imitation I had used several years before. I knocked: "Hello, honey, this is Al. . . ." I then broke into a few bars of "Mammy," and she opened the door and laughed. She looked around for Jolie, and when she didn't see him she went along with the gag.

For the next couple of weeks we spent most of our time together. One night, however, while having dinner at the Coconut Grove, Phil Baker walked up to our table, said hello to Lupe and then looked at me very seriously.

"Georgie, who was that blonde I saw you with last night? She was a beauty. . . ."

At this, Lupe's eyes caught on fire. She picked up a steak knife and speared the back of my left hand with it, impaling it to the table. I was speechless as a river of blood flowed out from *under* my palm onto the white tablecloth. Lupe was laughing like hell, and Phil took off for the hills.

After some first aid at the hotel, I went to the emergency hospital to have it cauterized after sending Lupe home in a cab. I didn't want this to get into the papers. The wound was dressed and was very painful. I still have the scar.

The next day I received the biggest brush-off anyone has ever received. Lupe was supposed to dine with me and patch up the difficulty that Phil had caused by his tasteless gag. She was due to arrive at 6:30. When 8:30 rolled around, I called her house and Lupe's lovely old mother answered the telephone.

"Who dis?" she asked.

"This is Georgie, George Jessel. Where is Lupe?"

"Oh, Lupe no here . . ."

"Did she leave any message for me?"

"Yes," replied the old lady. "Lupe say for me to tell you goodbye. No bananas today."

A "banana" to Lupe referred to that certain part of a man's anatomy. That was the end of my romance with Lupe Velez and Jolie had the last laugh. Or did he?

I learned later that when Jolson once started to criticize me in front of Lupe, she defended me with the remark, "At least he's a better lay than you are, Jolie." It was a real put down for Jolie and he never saw Lupe again.

*   *   *

While on the subject of Jolie (again), this might be a good time to talk about him at length. As you already know, I had known Jolie for many years, ever since our first meeting in San Francisco with Eddie Cantor. Jolie, I will say here and now, was truly one of the greatest entertainers America has ever produced. But offstage he was completely different.

I honestly lamented the passing of this great, great dynamic personality and talent and his impact on the theater; during my eulogy of Jolie I never ventured much about the man himself. For Jolie, too, like most men of extraordinary ability, was a man with many idiosyncrasies, and nobody got under his skin.

As I explained earlier, I met Jolson for the first time when I was eleven years old in San Francisco. He was already a star at the Winter Garden and across America.

Several years intervened, and it was not until 1919 that we met again on a first name basis. He was touring the country in a play called *Big Boy*, and I had a vaudeville act, *Georgie Jessel's Troubles*. If business was good, and it always was with Al, unless he ran into a slow night in Syracuse or a snowstorm in Des Moines, and if the stock market was up and he was winning the card games with his cronies, he was in a good humor.

He loved to talk a lot about the "old times" and old-timers, and he particularly got a great kick out of it when I would give imitations of such comedians as Harry Cooper, a famous actor who appeared on the stage as an old Jewish man. He had a long beard, wore a derby on his head, and sang in a rich, high tenor that was always a surprise to the audience. The first words of his old songs went: "In the green fields of Virginia / In the vale of Shenandoah . . ." if you can imagine such corny lyrics—but it was the style of the day.

Al would get such a charge out of my mimicry that I might be playing in Spokane and the phone would ring from Norfolk, Virginia, or some other such backwater, and Louis Epstein, Jolson's manager and devoted servant for many years, would get on and say in a very perfunctory manner, "Al wants to hear a few bars of Harry Cooper."

I would sing the few bars, and Eppy would close the conversation with, "Al says thanks and he will see you in New York."

This happened once or twice a week for a whole season. I was glad I wasn't paying the telephone bills.

But you can't say that Al was egocentric. Most men love themselves. I believe it was Oscar Wilde (or was it Ed Sullivan?) who said, "To love oneself is the beginning of a life-long romance."

Egocentric is too small a word for Jolson. Nature had somehow contrived him to be particularly immune to anyone else's pains and problems, so that he was only affected by what was happening to him at any particular moment. I can't believe he wanted to be like that, but nevertheless he was. As in the truthful portrayal of his life story on the screen, he was only content while singing and acknowledging applause. The rest of the time he was chafing at the bit while getting ready to go on; if he was not "on," he was disconsolate and miserable to be around.

The word *failure* in connection with anything he had to do was something he never uttered. At a horse race, in the stock market, at the ball game, you would always hear Jolie had a winner, even if you knew he hadn't. I remember once we went to the races at Belmont Park on Long Island. We came late, just as the first race was over, and sat down to have a sandwich. They were just putting up the numbers of the three first-race money horses.

A man passed us by and said to Jolie, "Did you have the winner, Al?"

Jolie characteristically replied, "I didn't bet much here, but I bet a big chunk with Sleepy Joe in Cincinnati."

"Well, you got a good price," replied the tout, "she was eight to one."

Al whispered to me, "Find out who won . . . I don't know what goat he's talking about."

While at the track, I walked around, listening to tipsters, watching people bet, watched and wagered on the races from several different boxes, and didn't get back to Jolie until the last race.

"Al, how did you do?" I queried, never expecting a straight answer.

"Never had a loser. You know I started off good with the first race—that eight to one shot!"

Right after the stock market crash, when I was wiped out of $400,000, I met him again. Cantor had also lost a bundle and almost every one of our friends had gone broke.

"I was lucky," said Al, not commiserating with us at all. "I sold everything the day before the crash."

After one of Jolie's marriages, which was a highly romantic episode, he and some of his cronies came to my dressing room at the theater where I was playing in *The War Song*. I asked him about his lady fair, how she was feeling, the usual niceties between friends.

In typical Jolson fashion, he answered me. "I don't know how she is."

"But, Al," I replied, surprised, "How can you say that? You've just come back from your honeymoon in Europe. Aren't you in love?"

Without batting an eyelid, Jolie looked at me deadly serious: "What love? Who wants to go to Europe alone?"

He wouldn't even admit to me, or even to himself, that he could love somebody more than himself.

During the intervals when he was a bachelor, we used to drive to Atlantic City for weekends. One night we were the judges at a Charleston contest and awarded the prizes to two young ladies—a Ruby Stevens and a girl called Mae Clarke. Al was quite taken by this Ruby Stevens. She was young, she could dance, she was pretty—and she later changed her name to Barbara Stanwyck. She had more authority and carriage than the average Charleston dancer of the day by far. It was obvious she could be a star one day.

We rode in the wheelchairs along the boardwalk at night. I, as per custom, started reciting those damn "Indian Love Lyrics" to Mae Clarke, but Jolie's way of wooing Ruby was typical.

"Honey, it's a funny thing, your name being Stevens. That's the name of the president of one of my banks that I got six million dollars in."

Ruby, smart girl that she was, knew how to handle him, but she was always upstaged at the end. I remember one telephone conversation they had as related later to me by Ruby. "I just got a letter from my aunt in Washington, D.C. Do you mind if I read it?"

"Go ahead," condescended Al, "I just bought ten thousand shares of American Tel and Tel . . ."

Miss Stevens, while quite flattered by Jolson's interest in her, did not go completely overboard. This, despite the fact that Al made several weekend trips to Atlantic City just to see her. He had a suite at the Ritz-Carlton in New York and I had an adjoining room. One morning I opened a telegram that had been shoved under my door. Naturally, I opened it. The contents didn't surprise me when I realized it was for Jolie and not me.

> Dear Al. Thanks for the flowers. If you are coming this weekend to see me, please don't. I have to keep other engagements. Fondly, Ruby.

I resealed the missive and slipped it under the door to Al's living room. While we were having breakfast I asked him if we were going to Atlantic City that weekend.

"No. It wouldn't be fair to Ruby keeping her stuck on me when I'm only kidding her. I just got a telegram from her saying that if I don't come down this weekend she'll just die. So, I just wired her back that I can't make it!"

Jolie could be terribly kind and terribly cruel to those who served him. You were his pal one moment, and the next a complete stranger working for him. The last few years most people would say of Al, "Isn't he getting mellow." But he was not getting mellow, he was just getting older.

At a dinner given for me after I had functioned at more than a dozen in honor of him, Al came on, made a speech, and then sang several songs to the delight of the audience. And then, just to make it tougher for me, who had to make the last speech of the evening, he said, "Folks, I'll stay on all night if you want me."

Furious, I jumped up and said, "No, you won't—this is my dinner and you can sit down now."

Fellows who are not in the know say he loved me. He didn't. He respected my ability to speak and recognized the fact that, having read a great deal, nine chances out of ten I would know what I was talking about.

No one will ever be able to understand that in his will he left great sums of money to colleges and organizations with which he had no association or admiration for. This is something to conjure with. But more so! The fact that the two men in whose arms he practically breathed his last breath on earth—one who had been with him over thirty-five years, the other not so long a time, but who toured the encampments with him all over the world and acted as his buddy and accompanist, and even his musical director—to these men with whom he played cards nightly, who rubbed his back for him, dined with him, took his gals home for him, visited his relatives as a surrogate for him, served him like loving brothers as well as if he had been a Roman emperor and they his slaves, *he left nothing.*

Not even a token of a tiny ring or a cufflink, a pin or a portrait or even a photograph. Even his music arranger and warm confidant for twenty years, who was also at his death bed, did not receive a farthing or a small remembrance. He left all his jewels, from beautiful black pearls down to a most masculine set of cufflinks, to people who were practically strangers to him, and more importantly, who needed none of these gifts.

Yet, despite the fact that these three old buddies of his were anything but rich, it was being completely forgotten without a one-line remembrance for faithful service that broke their hearts—not the monetary or material consideration.

What cruel twist was there in his last gesture of showing that no pal or relative meant anything to him? No one will ever know.

Yet, even today I miss him—and find that, despite everything, including the many cruel things that he did to me and said to me, I miss him. The way Jolie took the motion picture version of *The Jazz Singer* away from me, a show I made famous on Broadway and across the country, is a story I have already told.

He also stated long before he passed on that he didn't want me to eulogize him. It took the late Johnny Hyde, Marilyn Monroe's mentor and sometime paramour, who represented Al in several ventures, Ben Holzman, and the entire gang at the William Morris Agency, to convince his sweet widow, Erle, that the theatrical profession had chosen me to speak. He didn't even want me at the finish. Just as, at the height of his success, when nothing could possibly affect him, he hated to hear about anyone else making a hit, from a trained dog act on a dingy stage in Peoria to a fat soprano at the Met.

Yet, I miss him. For he was so good to look at—and he seemed so strong and such an impregnable fortress.

And I forgive him for many things.

As someone once said of Tchaikovsky, "He is a snob," to which another replied, "Yes, but, God, what beautiful music he writes."

So, of Jolie, he was cruel most of the time . . . But, God, what a great artist he was!

* * *

Following the Velez romance and the windup of my Tiffany-Stahl commitment, I returned to New York and went to see Hecht's play in rehearsal. I had never met him and was looking forward to doing so. In my mind Hecht was one of our greatest writers. I had pictured him in my mind as being a very esthetic looking man, the type who wore a flowing black Windsor tie. As I entered the stalls, Lewis motioned me to sit down next to a man chewing on a cigar and wearing a loud red tie and red shirt that could have been used as a stage curtain for a troupe of gay midgets.

I sat through almost a whole act of the play, and I thought it daffy to say the least. When the curtain fell and the last line was spoken by the keeper of the insane asylum, Lewis turned to me and asked me what I thought of it.

"Well, my honest opinion is that when the keeper comes in,

instead of coming for the characters of the play, he ought to ask for you and Hecht and take you both back to the asylum instead."

Lewis hurriedly introduced me to the character in the red shirt and tie. It was Ben. Despite the *faux pas* on my part, Hecht and I immediately got together for the dramatization of *Private Jones*. Our new title was *The War Song*, and after a couple of weeks, Hecht felt he could not collaborate with me because I talked almost as much as he did. We called it off although remaining on friendly terms.

The War Song finally reached the stage as the joint effort of Sam and Bella Spewack and myself. But we did discover that *Private Jones* was of no use to us at all. We had an entirely new story, with tragedy and low comedy too close together for stage success. Also, the Spewacks, being young and new to the theater, listened to everybody's advice about changes, as did I. The play opened in New York, got mixed notices, played ten weeks, and then went on tour. Because of my earlier success in the same theaters while appearing in *The Jazz Singer*, we did great business. In four weeks in Chicago we played to over $100,000. I don't believe any other drama until after the war, and with one star, if I may be so modest, ever equaled this business. In the play with me, however, were many young people who became important theatrical and motion picture figures: Gene Raymond, Lola Lane, William Gargan, and Shirley Booth.

While touring with *The War Song*, Tiffany-Stahl decided they could not release the last picture I had made for them, *Lucky Boy*. Silent films had lost their appeal, but they offered to give me the negative and pay all the expenses for me to make some sound tracks for the picture, incorporate songs wherever I could, and then they would release it. They also offered to give me twenty-five percent of the profits.

Al Lewis and Milford, who was now my manager, took a look at the film and convinced me that it did not have a chance, even if the whole Metropolitan Opera Company made sound tracks for it.

"But," said Milford, "tell them you will put a week in on it in New York for $20,000 cash, no profits, and with the $20,000 in front. They won't agree and that will be the end of that."

To our great surprise they did accept the terms, and with a

camera, sound apparatus, a few gags, and a very small series of sets, we went to work in two rooms at 411 Fifth Avenue. We interpolated five songs, one of which I wrote with L. Wolfe Gilbert and Abel Baer, "My Mother's Eyes," which eventually sold over two million copies of sheet music. For the last scene of the picture, which was the finale of a musical play, we hired the National Theater and a full company of actors on the stage, as well as three or four hundred extras for the audience.

When we were finished, *Lucky Boy*, with its synthetic interpolations, cost about $90,000 altogether, including the cost of the original silent version and my additional $20,000. It was not a very good picture, but it eventually grossed nearly a million dollars. Had I taken the twenty-five percent of the profits, I would have had $200,000 or thereabouts instead of the $20,000. And I might have been able to keep that nearly quarter million because it would have taken some time to collect it all. I immediately "invested" the twenty grand in more stocks with the well-meaning advice of a guy named Cantor and his bankers.

After the preview of *Lucky Boy*, Tiffany-Stahl offered me another deal to do a full-length sound film. They purchased a story I had written, "Dandy Dan," a gangster tale laid in New York. One or two pictures of this genre had been highly successful at the box office. Because I knew a great deal about this subject—in fact, I knew nearly all of the New York and Chicago mobsters intimately —my story was authentic. It had a good part for me, too—that of a piano player unwittingly brought in to play and sing while a guy was being deep sixed. The piano player, of course, was the fall guy for the hit.

Winfield Sheehan, general manager of the Fox Film Corporation, learned of the grosses of *Lucky Boy* and asked for a meeting with Al Lewis, now with Fox, Milford, sans mustache but with a new, blonde wife, and myself. Sheehan told me Fox was interested in making three pictures before I explained I had a contract and had sold a story to Tiffany-Stahl. Sheehan said they would find a way to work that out with them. I then outlined the story of "Dandy Dan," and he agreed that it would be my first picture for Fox.

Milford and I talked privately and I told him what I wanted.

"Try to get $50,000 for the three pictures, to be done in thirty weeks. Then I can play a few weeks of vaudeville and won't have to worry about a play for next year. Also," I added for good measure, "let them buy back the story from Tiffany-Stahl for more than the $2,500 we got for it, but make the check out to me so we can make a profit on that as well."

A week later, Milford came to me with an astonishing contract, which included the following terms: I was to get $150,000 for three pictures. (Milford had misunderstood me and thought I meant $50,000 for each film.) The contract also included five round-trip railroad fares to the coast and back, and $10,000 for "Dandy Dan," a profit of $7,500, which we split with T-S. It turned out I was to get over $150,000 for three pictures and I had only asked for $52,500. Milford was learning—fast.

A week later I played a week of vaudeville in Chicago, and to get more color on gangdom, I set out to meet "all the boys." Through a contact I had, I found myself dining with Al Capone himself. I met him in his office at the Lexington Hotel. There were no guns on his desk, contrary to what the papers had been reporting for years. We had supper at the Midnight Frolics—Capone, Teddy Newberry, and myself. No bodyguards were evident, no armored cars or any of the other trappings most newspapers of the era had given Capone credit for over the years.

During dinner, Capone told me of a very amusing incident that had happened earlier that winter at his home in Palm Island, Florida. This home, by the way, again contrary to the newspaper reports, was a very small house. Al also had a 38-foot power boat, the *Oozer*. Both boat and house were always photographed so that the house looked like Buckingham Palace and the boat like the *Leviathan*, thus perpetuating the myth of Capone.

Al asked a prominent comedian, then appearing in Miami, to dine with him one evening. The comic arrived, very frightened, and immediately began to entertain, not stopping until he had sung over twenty-four songs and told over a hundred jokes. After thinking about this story of Al's for several months, I was never able to understand how a man with such nerve on his radio show, and the father of five grown daughters, could have been so scared of a man like Al Capone. I kidded Eddie Cantor about it for years.

Dining with Capone, however, was also very important to me for another very good reason. In the Chicago of those days, actors and performers were being shaken down for almost any reason —generally protection money. Rudy Vallee, Lou Holtz, Georgie Price, Ted Healey, all paid off for this so-called protection. If they didn't, they were told, they would get hurt. "Remember Joe E. Lewis?" was the usual admonition. Lewis, of course, had had his throat cut from ear to ear a year earlier because he refused to work in a mob-owned Chicago club as a greeter and comic.

In fact, it was during this current engagement that I agreed to appear at a benefit for Lewis to cover his medical expenses. Capone raised no objection when I asked his okay. However, this affair could have had disastrous consequences for me.

*   *   *

I have always had a great penchant for the sauce and have concocted many varieties of highballs and mixed drinks over the years. But very few people know how the Bloody Mary came to be. Today, it is one of the most popular "morning after" or "hang-over" cures there is, as well as a companion for Sunday brunch.

In 1927, I was living in Palm Beach, or on a short visit, I don't remember which, where nearly every year I captained a softball team for a game against the elite of Palm Beach such as the Woolworth Donohues, the Al Vanderbilts, the Reeves, and their ilk. My team was made up of rag-tag New York café society. Because I had been around Broadway and baseball characters, I managed to slip in a ringer now and again. (We generally won.)

On this particular trip I brought along Buddy Adler, a semi-pro on Long Island and a shoe salesman during the week. Buddy was later to become production head at 20th Century-Fox and marry Anita Louise. Both of them, unfortunately, are now dead. The proceeds of our, shall we say, friendly wagers on the games, went to a charity for underprivileged children. Adler hit a home run with the bases loaded, and we won the game and collected several thousand dollars in bets.

There was a famous hangout in Palm Beach at the time run by Paddy La Maze, a former ball player himself. To the winners, he let them drink all the champagne they could take; the losers, beer.

Following the game, Adler (who was hung like a bull, generally came along to try to find a rich dowager to marry but never did), myself, and a guy named Elliott Sperver, a Philadelphia playboy, went to La Maze's and started swilling champagne. We were still going strong at 8:00 A.M. the next morning. I had a 9:30 volleyball date with Al Vanderbilt. I was feeling no pain at all.

We tried everything to kill our hangovers and sober up. Then Charlie, the bartender, enjoying our plight, reached behind the bar.

"Here, Georgie, try this," he said, holding up a dusty bottle I had never seen before. "They call it *vodkee*. We've had it for six years and nobody has ever asked for it. . . ."

I looked at it, sniffed it. It was pretty pungent and smelled like rotten potatoes. "Hell, what have we got to lose? Get me some Worcestershire sauce, some tomato juice, and lemon; that ought to kill the smell," I commanded Charlie. I also remembered that Constance Talmadge, destined to be my future sister-in-law, always used to drink something with tomatoes in it to clear her head the next morning and it always worked—at least for her.

"We've tried everything else, boys, we might as well try this," I said as I started mixing the ingredients in a large glass. After we had taken a few quaffs, we all started to feel a little better. The mixture seemed to knock out the butterflies.

Just at that moment, Mary Brown Warburton walked in. A member of the Philadelphia branch of the Wanamaker department store family, she liked to be around show business people and later had a fling with Ted Healey, the comic. She had obviously been out all night because she was still dressed in a beautiful white evening dress.

"Here, Mary, take a taste of this and see what you think of it."

Just as she did, she spilled some down the front of her white evening gown, took one look at the mess, and laughed. "Now, you can call me Bloody Mary, George!"

From that day to this, the concoction I put together at La Maze's has remained a Bloody Mary with very few variations. Charlie pushed it every morning when "the gang" was under the weather.

* * *

Now, about a year later, the benefit for Joe E. Lewis was to be held at the Oriental Theater and I was sitting in my hotel room with Ted Healey before leaving for the theater. Ted, as usual, was slightly inebriated. He happened to pick up a copy of a Chicago paper and read an item in Winchell's column. It said that I had named the Bloody Mary after Ted's then steady girl, Mary Brown Warburton.

Ted turned white. "What the hell are you doing making a pass at my girl, you son of a bitch," he yelled. And just as he did, he pulled out a pistol and tried to shoot me. I ducked and the shot missed, but as the pistol went off within a foot of my right ear, I was completely deaf for a week. I had a hell of a job doing the benefit that night.

But at least now you know the origin of the Bloody Mary, and I believe it was *Esquire* magazine who finally gave me credit for it many, many years ago.

Too bad I can't collect royalties on it. In fact, I have never even received a case of vodka from any of the distillers for helping to make vodka the most popular, er, beverage, in the United States today.

The night after the benefit and two days after my dinner with Al, Hymie Weiss, the toughest of the Chicago hoods, came to see me and pass the word that I was "okay" with the mob and would never be bothered anywhere in the country for shakedown money.

I was a bit dubious about Hymie's assurances a week later when his body, riddled by machine gun bullets, was found in a Chicago alley. He had been taken for a one-way ride. I felt maybe I was next, and that evening it appeared that way.

Capone, in what turned out to be a stroke of the infinite wisdom of the gangster mind, had one of his boys telephone me to say that some of the boys were giving a dinner for a Tom Malloy on the West Side. Al would like me to give a speech even though he would not be there. I was also told that there would be more than a thousand people present; they turned out to be the *crème de la crème* of Chicago mobdom and labor union chiefs. I said I was very tired —it was already past midnight—and since I didn't know Mr. Malloy, it would be almost impossible for me to talk about him. I also had a young chorus girl in the room with me.

"Put on your tuxedo, Georgie, right now, and we'll meet ya in the lobby. Otherwise, we'll come up and getcha!" In the Chicago of the late 1920s, one did not refuse such a command performance. Nevertheless, I had Hymie on my mind. I was dressed and downstairs in five minutes, telling my young lady friend languishing in a bubble bath to wait for me.

Once in the car, I looked at my inscrutable companions and tried to make conversation. "Well, boys, what can I say about Mr. Malloy, and what has he done recently?"

"What's it to you," a fellow with no nose and one ear muttered.

I could extract very little information, except that I was to make a "swell speech" as Malloy was "a swell guy." When I arrived in the room, it was absolute bedlam; you couldn't cut the cigar smoke with a knife. I was rushed to the speaker's table and introduced to "the boys."

Everyone was drunk and you couldn't hear a word. I spoke anyway, never one to turn down an opportunity to make a speech—especially a command performance such as this.

"Gentlemen," I started, "this is a moment to remember." It was for me, anyway. "This is also a memory to conjure with. How silly it is of me, humble minstrel passing through your great city, to speak of the great virtues of your guest of honor, Tom Malloy! For who was it that crossed the Delaware? Who was it who freed the slaves? Who was it who charged up San Juan Hill? Who was it who invented electricity?"

I was reverting to an old Jimmy Walker ploy, who, if he didn't know anything about the group he was addressing, would go down the list of the ethnic population of New York until he hit the nerve. I had learned my lesson well because "the boys" started to listen.

"Perhaps it was not your Mr. Malloy," I concluded, "but I know that if given the opportunity he would have done all these wonderful things. I thank you!"

I found out later that Malloy was the head of the Theater Projectionists Union in Chicago, and later in the country.

The boys took me back to the car and gave me a case of whiskey and then drove me back to the hotel. I believe it was the first time in American gangdom that a guy was taken for a ride and not bumped off. Capone only wanted to let me know that what Hymie Weiss had told me was true; I was okay with the mob.

Following this incident, and after closing on Saturday night, I rushed out to the coast. Anticipating all the money I was to get, thanks to Milford's naiveté, I sent for my mother, Milford's mother, Florence, her mother and father, and a few more relatives. I rented a huge house in Beverly Hills, complete with swimming pool, tennis court, and bar. I then went to the Fox Studio on Western Avenue and Sunset Boulevard.

The first thing I learned was that my gangster picture was off, but another vehicle was "being prepared for me" with the title *Love, Live and Laugh.* I was not to play a Broadwayite, but a blind, Italian soldier, if you please, who played an accordion and sang in the damn trenches. I was later to switch to German when taken to a prison camp. I did the best I could with this shoddy and horrible material.

Had they used any common sense, the picture might have made a little money. It grossed almost half a million and should have cost around $300,000 to make. For one scene, supposedly the Bay of Naples, the company sent a whole troupe of cameramen to Italy. They came back with a few hundred feet of film and shots that resembled the East River on a murky winter day. We finally photographed the Bay of Naples in miniature at the studio. With other unnecessary expenses, the cost of the film was over $800,000.

After completion of the picture, I returned to New York, not only for the preview at the Roxy Theater, but also to be the guest of honor at a dinner given by the Jewish Theatrical Guild of America. Tammany Hall supported it enthusiastically. In attendance was the governor, the mayor, Jimmy Walker, and most of the leading members of the theatrical profession. On my right was William Fox himself, my boss. He made a great speech, saying how happy he was because of my association with his company on the coast. It turned out to be the latter-day "vote of confidence," which usually means you are out.

Two days later I returned to the coast. The day I left, the first big stock market crash occurred. Everything I had earned was in stocks, at least the surplus. And half of them were on fifty percent margin. By the time the train arrived in Buffalo, only seven hours from New York, I was half broke. By the time I reached Pasadena, I was just hanging on.

I arrived at the studio, undaunted by my losses in the market. I felt I would be greeted by a long-term contract after that speech by William Fox. I was immediately called into the executive offices. I was told they would like to make a settlement with me and not make the last two pictures. They felt they did not have the right stories, but if they did get them, possibly the following year, they would send for me.

I was willing to defer the contract, but not to tear it up. "Gentlemen, there isn't anything you can do to me that will make me give up the money you owe me. You can use all your Hollywood tricks, get me down here at five o'clock in the morning, make me up as a pickle or an umbrella cover, but I want that dough.

"It isn't my fault that you geniuses of the western world hired Georgie Jessel and then hid him behind blacked-out eyes and an oversized accordion and made him sing in four or five foreign languages. I want my money."

With that, I stormed out of the office, rushed back to my Beverly Hills mansion, where my aunt, mother, and all the other relatives were gaily eating salami by the swimming pool.

"Everybody pack," I shouted.

"What happened?" asked my mother, shocked.

"The Egyptians are coming," I told her, not knowing what else to say. It took me a few days to get my money, which was paid in cash. I went to the studio every day and no one would talk to me, which was customary, and still is, under the same circumstances.

My whole entourage was packed and ready to go, and I even made Fox give me those five railroad tickets to New York as part of the settlement.

When I went to get the necessary papers and cash from the bookkeeper, I rushed past half a dozen secretaries, into the private office of Sheehan, who was in a meeting with several sycophants.

"Gentlemen, I am leaving for New York in ten minutes. I would like to have any one of you spell 'cat' for me before I go. If you feel you are not up to it right now, we will meet at another time when I can coach you in it. Goodbye!"

The settlement from Fox was all I had left. The stock market had wiped me out to the tune of $400,000. With the money from Fox, I went into partnership with John Golden and produced a version of *Joseph and His Brethren* staged by old friend, George S. Kaufman and myself.

Golden's intentions were good, but he was in Palm Beach. His office arranged to have the play open on the same night as the great French success *Topaz*. This meant that I would get few, if any, of the important critics to attend the opening night. And the satire of *Joseph* was something that needed the first string if it was to succeed on Broadway.

The opening night saw a strange audience. Very few of the carriage trade came to see us. They were all at the the Music Box acclaiming Frank Morgan in *Topaz*. My audience consisted of relatives and a gallery filled with East Side folk who had cherished *The Jazz Singer*. They had come to the theater expecting to see a dramatic and certainly orthodox portrayal of the biblical Joseph. They were sadly disappointed, for mine was a streamlined Joseph, kidding about his forefathers and mentioning Abraham, Isaac, and Jacob in a light and even joking manner. George S. Kaufman had done a beautiful directorial job and the critic, later actor, Robert Benchley thought it was the finest performance I had ever given, even better than *The Jazz Singer*. The second string newspaper critics damned it with faint praise. Nevertheless, nobody came to see it.

There I was, playing a role almost as long as Hamlet's, making many costume changes, from tattered rags to the coat of many colors, wearing bronze makeup over my entire body, shouting and screaming and pounding on the door of Pharaoh's palace, entreating him to let me come in and clarify his dream, and with every performance, personally losing about $600. I called John Golden, and he told me he would go along with me if I liked, but to use my own judgment. I closed the show that week. The large cast, including Ferdinand Gottschalk, Douglas Dumbrille, Ara Gerald, Ann Tieman, and fifty other players, were very sad because they liked the play very much. Hating to go through a series of sad goodbyes, I did something that I don't think had ever been done before, or even since, in the theater. Attired in my coat of many colors, I kept the curtain up at the end of the play, walked down to the footlights, and made a speech to what audience there was.

"Ladies and gentlemen," I said, "the curtain shall soon fall on this play for the last time. The clothing, the scenery you see on the stage, will soon be in the warehouse. If you listen, you can even hear the horses of Cain neighing impatiently at the stage door. I like this play, and so do the members of my company, and we like each other. The closing of a play is like the end of a world. Even among actors who don't like each other, a closing finds them saying goodbye tearfully, hoping they meet again with a happier manuscript. So, because of the sentimental feeling and because I have gone through so much with this show, I don't feel strong enough to have any more emotional scenes about it. I'm taking the liberty of saying goodbye to the play, its players, in front of you, the audience, for the actors will not cry, no more than they would sneeze, under these circumstances. Thank you."

With that, I motioned for the curtain to fall. I stepped over the footlights, makeup, robes, and all, hailed a cab in front of the theater, and went home.

I decided then and there I would not go on the stage again until I found something that had a chance to become a popular success. I was through with highbrow plays. I would produce. Yes, that's what I would do, and I did. I arranged a lease on the New Yorker Theater on Fifty-fourth Street. I had a great idea.

The eminent Jewish tragedian, Jacob Adler, had many children; so many, it was once said, that while walking through the streets of Bucharest, he bought a newspaper from a little boy, looked at him, and said, "What was your mother's name?"

When the child answered, "Anna," the actor said, "Here is an extra coin. I am your father."

True or not, his children, as well as all the near and distant branches of the family, had and have great talent. I arranged to get as many of the Adlers together as I could—Luther, Jack, Celia, Frances, Frances's husband Joseph Shoengold, Abe Adler, Charlie, and two or three more. I brought them to Broadway in a Yiddish version of the famous German play, *The Five Frankfurters*, which was the saga of the German branch of the Rothschild family.

While this show was in rehearsal, I purchased a play, still using some of the $100,000 settlement money from Fox, called *This Man's Town* by Willard Robertson. I cast Pat O'Brien, Constance Cummings, Mary Howard, and several others. This was a play in one scene that took place in a lunch wagon in the small hours of the morning. Because I was doing two plays at the same time, I left the entire staging of *This Man's Town* to the very fine actor, Lester Lonergan. I had full confidence in his ability because of his association with *The Road to Rome* and several other hits. But at the first performance in Newark, I was sure that Lonergan had the wrong slant on what the author had intended, and what I wanted to see on the stage. This was a comedy about people who wanted a hamburger and a cup of coffee; the murders and intrigues were of secondary importance. Mr. Lonergan had staged it the other way, as a melodrama. Because of my great respect for Lester, and because I was much younger, I had a tough time easing him out, even though I paid him off in full. I set about restaging the play myself and did a pretty good job. A few days later I was offered a piece of the great success *Street Scene*, then in rehearsal, for a piece of *This Man's Town*. I didn't take it, and I made ready to bring my show into New York. Before the curtain rose, Lonergan went backstage to see the cast, without my permission. He advised them, I was told later, to protect themselves by playing as he had directed.

"After all, Jessel is only a song and dance man. He knows nothing about the legitimate theater. . . ."

And that's the kind of performance the actors gave the opening night—half my way, and half Lonergan's. By the end of the second act, there was also half an audience. Before the play was over, I sent the stage manager a note to put up the closing sign three days later.

The Adlers' show folded, too. I got drunk, and then became sick with a nervous stomach. I wished Joseph had never been born. I was fed up with the Frankfurters.

I was ready to leave "This Man's Town. . . ."

9

Europe—In Happier Times

IT was March 27, and I suddenly realized that I was more than a year late for my date with Lita Chaplin in London. Through Winchell's column, I discovered that Lita was again in New York. I called her at the Waldorf and she told me that she, too, had :"missed the boat" but would be leaving in a few days. We made a date to meet at the Savoy in two weeks.

Florence saw me off and said she might surprise me in Paris. "I've never been out of the country. Perhaps we can find what we've lost in Paris, George," she told me as she left my stateroom to go ashore.

I met Lita at the Savoy as planned, and we took up where we had left off the previous year. Our rooms at the Savoy adjoined; you could not check into a hotel in those days as "Mr. and Mrs." as you can today with no questions asked. (In fact, I might add here that it is my observation that the marriage vows today, in or out of show business, consist of four words: "Your house or mine?")

I spent the daytime hours in and out of the Old Bailey, paying homage to the bust of Sir George Jessel, running over to the Cheshire Cheese, drinking ale from the same mugs that had been hoisted by Dickens, Dr. Johnson and his Boswell, and for a while forgot my troubles at home. Lita spent the daytime hours shopping and visiting old friends.

It was time to leave for Paris, and Lita and I made a date to meet at the Georges V within a few days for supper. Full of romance in Paris in the spring, I arrived at the appointed hour and inquired of the *concièrge* as to the whereabouts of Lita.

"Madame Chaplin is in the dining room, monsieur." And there she was, lovelier than ever at a table for two, but my chair was occupied by Georges Carpentier, who had recently fought Jack Dempsey in New York. I felt he was no match for me and decided it would be more prudent to write some letters in my room.

But later on that evening I met up with old friends Rupert Hughes and Marc Connolly at the *Tour d'Argent*, where I had gone for some duck à l'orange to assuage my ruffled plumage, to hell with the duck. We agreed over dinner to make a motor trip to Versailles the next day and stop for lunch at the Four Roads of the King, a very romantic restaurant so named because Louis XIV would often stop to dine and then decide which of the four roads he would take to which palace. I had been singing to Rupert and Marc as we entered the restaurant, and the old proprietor beamed when he saw me. I couldn't figure out why.

He insisted upon waiting on us himself and asked if we would drink a bottle of wine "on the house." (That didn't happen very often in France, and still doesn't.) When we finished our delicious meal, he apologetically announced that, if things were better, he would have loved to have me and my friends as his guests.

"Not at all," I said, a little bewildered by this man's admiration for me. *Private Izzy Murphy* had played a few weeks in Paris, and I thought perhaps he just might have seen it. As we reached for our hats, the old man said, in his best "touristy English," would I please do him one favor? Would I meet his wife and daughter? Without waiting for me to reply, he called to the kitchen, and out came a stoutish woman with a young daughter, both perspiring from the heat of the kitchen, the mother wiping her hands on her already very grubby apron.

The simple little daughter, blushing furiously, rushed over to me. They spoke no English, but the daughter said something which, translated, meant, would I sign her schoolbook. Of course I would. As I reached for a pen, the proprietor looked at me and smiled. "Oh, Monsieur Jolson, we see your picture 'Sonny Boy' ten times, and when you sing to zee baby, my wife, she cry, I cry, we all cry. Oh, Monsieur Jolson, you are wonderful."

Whereupon I sang a full chorus of "Sonny Boy" and signed the damn schoolbook "Al Jolson." I dared Rupert or Marc to mention it again on the way to Versailles, even though they found it hard to keep a straight face.

That night we all went to Joselli's Royal Box near the Madeleine and an offshoot of that night was to occur five years later. During the evening, I gravitated toward the piano with Rupert and Marc and joined Dick Rodgers and Larry Hart as well as several other entertainers. An American sister act, whom I shall call Billie and Mae, then appearing at the Alhambra Music Hall, took a shine to me and joined me around the piano of the theatrical hangout. As Rupert, Marc, Larry, and Dick got up to leave about 3:00 A.M., Mae grabbed my arm.

"Where are you going?" she asked. "Why don't you come back to our apartment and have a nightcap?"

Naturally, I wasn't about to turn down that invitation. Arriving at their flat on the Rue Caumartin, Billie turned to Mae as soon as we were inside. "Where are the cards?"

"Hey, wait a minute, girls," said I, naively, "I didn't come here at three in the morning to play cards!"

Mae laughed, looking at Billie as though for approval. "We know that, but we're going to play a hand of poker, and the one who wins gets you for the night!"

Mae won with a full house, and we retired to her bedroom in the middle of which was a huge brass bed, the kind you sink into three feet before touching bottom. As I sank into Mae's bed, I laughed to myself and thought that this was the first time I ever got laid as the result of a poker hand.

Mae and I had a marvelous go-round for two or three hours, and when I returned to the hotel, Rupert and Marc were just coming in and looked at me, rather knowingly I felt.

I never saw either Billie or Mae again. But five years later I received a letter in care of the theater in which I was appearing at the time. Mae had obviously taken the trouble to go through the New York papers—or the *New Yorker* magazine—to discover my whereabouts.

The letter surprised me, to say the least:

Dear George:

I doubt whether you remember me but we spent a few hours together in Paris about five years ago.

Since then, my sister [Billie] and I have retired and I am married to a very fine man from the Argentine. I just wanted you to know that you and I have a son born from that night who I named David.

I would appreciate it if you didn't try to find him—or me—because of my marriage.

Sincerely,
[Mae]*

The letter was postmarked from Buenos Aires but contained no return address.

Two days later, Florence arrived. Eager to give our marriage another try, particularly since my "romance" with Lita had gone bust, we set out for Paris from Cherbourg. Florence had brought along our dog, a cute but mean little bastard, a terrier she had rescued a couple of years earlier from an animal act that had found itself impoverished while on tour. She did everything she could to make him a good little dog, even reading him passages from the Scriptures. But "the hoont" had only one aim in life—to bite people. He demonstrated his ability on a French customs inspector and a train conductor. By the time we reached Paris, neither Florence nor I, nor the conductor, would go anywhere near that damn dog. She stuck him in his traveling cage and ignored him.

While I was in Paris, I did some research on a very famous performer at the *Comédie Française* in the 1800s, a Madame Rachel. She was famous for her beauty and as one of the greatest *tragediennes* the French theater has ever known. She also had affairs with Victor Hugo, Alexandre Dumas and his son, and Napoleon the Third. I had an idea in the back of my mind that her

---

*Because they may both still be alive, and certainly, I should think, my son, "Billie and Mae" are not their real names. "David" *is* my son's name in case he reads this and cares to find me. I would like to see him.

life would make a great musical for Broadway and, possibly, a motion picture.

I even went so far as to track down her burial place in the Père Lachaise cemetery. I did not know at the time she was an orthodox Jewess and would, therefore, be buried in the Jewish section. (To show how famous she was, there were reputed to be 25,000 people in her funeral *cortège*.) I finally found her buried under her family name of Felix next to a tomb with a huge Star of David on top. It was the final resting place of Pierre Du Pont, the great-grandfather of the founder of the Du Pont chemical dynasty in Delaware. Madame Rachel Felix was buried next to him.

Two days later we left for Berlin and the Adlon Hotel. Berlin was a wonderful city in those days. The people were gentle and kind, and the rumble of the murderous Nazi war machine, then starting in Munich, had not been heard of along the Unter den Linden. On our first night in Berlin, we spent a very pleasant evening at the Staats Opera House for a performance of *Tosca*.

After supper at the hotel, Florence retired to her Bible, and I decided to stay in the bar for a nightcap or two. I had no problem with the language, as I spoke and understood German. During the evening, I met up with a stoutish man with the very German name of Hugo, who turned out to be the Berlin representative of ASCAP.* We talked about the war and what it had done to the flower of German (and American and British) youth.

"Let's take a walk and I'll show you something," said Hugo. We left the Adlon and crossed the Kurfuerstendam. Directly opposite was a café called the El Dorado, the prototype for the café in *Cabaret*, and the original nightclub with telephones on the tables for "pick up" purposes. The club was full of queers and transvestites, lesbians and dikes. At the bar I spotted a large individual dressed as a woman. It was also obvious that "he" was in his cups by the way he was "pawing" at a blond young man standing next to him.

"There," said Hugo, pointing. "That is one of *our* tragedies of the war. He was one of our greatest fighter pilots and came out of

---

*The American Society of Composers, Authors and Publishers. Most of the music being played in Europe in those days was written by Americans, and someone to monitor the royalties was necessary.

the army a colonel. He dresses like that practically every night and either comes in here or walks the streets until he gets picked up. His name is Hermann Goering. . . ."

I learned later that there were many other future German (Nazi) "leaders" in the El Dorado that night. The blond young man being pawed by Goering, I learned from Hugo later, was Ernst Roehm, later to be leader of Hitler's Brown Shirts, Roehm's own little homosexual army made infamous during "The Night of the Long Knives" massacre several years later when Roehm's "army" was wiped out by the Gestapo upon the orders of Hitler.

I thought about the El Dorado a great deal after the war when Goering and his remaining cronies were sitting in the dock at Nuremberg. It pretty well summed up the perverted character of the Nazis.

After six more days in Berlin, Florence and I caught the Berlin-Venice Express for Italy. But our stay in the City of the Canals was to be short-lived.

On our second day in Venice, I received a cable from Billy Rose, who was not yet the Little Napoleon of Broadway. Would I be interested in going into a musical revue as costar with his then current wife Fannie Brice?

Needless to say, I was. A few days later we sailed on the *Majestic* from Cherbourg.

Our European jaunt was over; things hadn't changed much between Florence and myself.

10

Corned Beef, Roses, and Billy Rose

THE Billy Rose of the early thirties was not as smart nor as nice as he was later on in his career. He was one of the few men who became less egotistical by success. I learned that Billy was planning a very elaborate revue to be called *Billy Rose's Corned Beef and Roses*.

Actually, it was all being prepared under the guidance of Jed Harris—remember the "review" he had given me in Chicago years before?—who had already produced four or five dramatic successes on Broadway. As an act of friendship, he was going to help Billy do the revue—a business about which he knew nothing. Although Billy, Jed, and I liked each other, we started to fight like hell as soon as the contract was signed. I was reminded that I was just a performer in this show, and consequently they were not interested in my suggestions as to the production itself. This was very awkward for me since I had been either my own boss, author, or partner in everything I had ever done in show business—with the exception of a few lousy movies.

Finally, I was given a lyric to sing that took a rap at the Shuberts. Not only because the Shuberts were my friends, but because I didn't think it was funny, I refused to do the number and walked out of the theater. Rose took the matter to Actors Equity, and Eddie Cantor was called in to arbitrate. I went back to the show, but with the Shubert reference omitted.

The first thing a revue in those days needed was a routine. Something had to be going on in front of the curtain while the stage was being set for the full stage scene coming up. Little thought had been given to this during rehearsals—it was due to Billy's and Jed's lack of experience in this type of show.

A great deal of the material in the revue was great. It had more song hits than any other revue ever produced up to that time. "Cheerful Little Earful," "Just a Gigolo," "Would You Like to Take a Walk," "Million Dollar Baby," and many, many others still played today on many radio stations.

We were scheduled to open the following Monday in Philadelphia with a dress rehearsal to begin at 6:00 P.M. on Sunday night. On the train down, I entered the drawing room of the Messrs. Rose and Harris and again offered my services in helping "routine" the show. I was politely but firmly advised to tell my jokes, sing my songs, and do nothing else. They added that the advance sale in Philadelphia was tremendous. I was told I—or they—had nothing to worry about.

At the Sunday night dress, it became rather obvious that we were in no condition to open the following night. As a matter of fact, we did not open until three nights later, and Rose had to refund all the money for the tickets for the four cancelled performances.

There were stage waits of an hour and a half between scenes. During these waits, the forty chorus girls would lie around in their costumes while I did my best to give them a laugh or two. I would go to my dressing room and make up as Abe Lincoln, then as Theodore Roosevelt, and finally, at 5:00 A.M., I came down in the makeup of Professor Larbermarcher, a poor, half-blind European lecturer. This was a character I did rather frequently on my vaudeville tours. There was so much fun in this for the girls that Billy told me to add some more dialogue and he would get some funny pictures and, if possible, incorporate it into the show. I proved my point in a roundabout way and Billy kept his word. I was doing the same routine thirteen years later on radio and on the stage.

(When we got to New York, the critics, headed by old friend George Jean Nathan, said, "This is the world's funniest monologue.")

The show finally opened in Philadelphia, and although I was scheduled for four appearances during the show, I had to go on about twenty times to fill in the stage waits. Jed Harris, truly a genius in producing legitimate plays, now realized that a big, rough and tumble revue was not his oyster. He had spent six hours, for instance, getting the right blue light to shine on a table in one of the scenes.

The Philadelphia papers blasted the hell out of the show. Jed went back to New York, and Billy called a meeting of the authors and composers. We removed all the "artistic" numbers and ballets and replaced them with "socko"—to quote *Variety*—vaudeville specialties. James Barton and his famous drunk act, Borah Minnevitch and His Harmonica Rascals, Moss and Fontana, the dance team, and we added an extra song for little Hannah Williams. The title of the show was changed to *Sweet and Low,* and it opened in New York and became a huge success. Rose and Harris should have let me put my ideas into the show at the *start* of the production and they would have saved thousands.

I was very gay during the run of this musical, a hit show again and I was on top of the heap. I gave a lot of parties and I had a crush on little Hannah. But she was keeping company, as the saying went, with Roger Wolfe Kahn, the son of the famous banker. She was told by Fannie Brice that I was the last guy in the world anyone should fall in love with.

Fannie called me into her dressing room and told me what she had said to Hannah. "You know I'm right, Georgie. You would never be satisfied with one girl."

"Yes, I would," I told her. "But I know I will never get her." I then told Fannie about meeting Norma several years before.

"That's funny," replied Fannie, "Norma and I are great friends. You know she's separated from Joe and she's coming to New York this week? I just had a wire from her. . . ."

I felt a strange tingle at this information, and a few nights later I learned that Norma Talmadge was in the audience. Following the performance, Norma, I, and her great friend Jay Brennan, one of the real wits of those times in offstage conversation, had supper and sat and talked until the small hours. It was very evident to me that Norma was very much in love with her current leading man, Gilbert Roland.

She then added that she and Joe would be divorced as soon as they could get around to it. A day or two later, Norma had to leave for the coast for some retakes and I went to the station with her. A moment before the 20th Century pulled out of Grand Central, I held her hand.

"I wonder when I will see you again, Norma. . . ."

I then quoted a few lines from the current Broadway play *Tomorrow and Tomorrow*, which escape me at the moment. But Norma liked them and took a firm hold on my hand and whispered, "Perhaps, tomorrow and tomorrow. . . ."

That night I received a telegram from her reading simply,

Tomorrow and tomorrow. Love, Norma.

It was then I realized (and hoped) that this might be more than a passing fancy on her part and that her "romance" with Gilbert was merely infatuation.

Sweet and Low was set to go on tour, but because I wanted to return to the bigger money of vaudeville, I left the cast after twenty-three very successful weeks and played two weeks at the Palace. After this, I was booked for two weeks on the road.

With me on the bill were George Burns and Gracie Allen, then a small-time song and dance team. Gracie, now dead, had been playing straight roles in vaudeville skits, while Burns had been a hoofer. They had met while on tour, fallen in love, married, and were doing an act that had some possibilities. I spent every evening in their apartment or hotel room, and I came to realize that, while on stage Burns was timid, frightened, anything but sure of himself, offstage he was one of the funniest men I had ever known. I did everything to build up his self-confidence and to make him believe how funny he really was. To build up this feeling, I kept bringing people with me each evening such as Jimmy Walker, Pola Negri —with whom I had a short fling—George M. Cohan, Irving Berlin, Sam Harris, and every celebrity who came to town. They found themselves screaming with laughter at George's antics, his cracks and tongue-in-cheek remarks.

Eddie Cantor suddenly arrived from the coast. He had just

made a picture and was planning to spend the rest of the year in
New York concentrating on his Chase and Sanborn radio show.
Eddie and I had enjoyed playing benefits together around town,
and he had conceived the idea of arranging our own show for the
Palace. We would play two weeks, and if it was good, have a lot of
fun. We were both being bombarded with requests to play freebies
and they started to become irksome. They are still a scourge to the
theatrical profession.

Eddie and I finished laying out the show and immediately had
a prominent place in it for George and Gracie. We encountered
some difficulty with our booking office. Burns and Allen, we were
told, were "cute," but for such a dynamite show we would need a
"stronger act." That was unless Burns and Allen had something
stronger to offer, or something new. I went to bat for them and told
the booking office manager they had a new act, "a good one," I
added for good measure.

When we finally opened, Burns had incorporated ever so
many of his offstage cracks. Burns and Allen were a riotous hit;
they did their own act and appeared with Eddie and me in several
skits.

In the meantime, Gracie was being talked about all over town
as the sweetest, dumbest girl of the century. Later, Eddie Cantor
featured Burns and Allen on his radio show. A short time after the
Palace show, which, incidentally, lasted three months instead of
the hoped-for two weeks, Burns and Allen had their own radio
show. It became one of the highest rated shows on the air, rivaling
Jack Benny for ratings.

The engagement at the Palace was a great deal of fun and I was
very happy. I made the rounds of all the nightclubs every night,
planning new barbs for Cantor the following day. Despite the fact I
found little time for sleep, I was in the best of health. Cantor,
meanwhile, was going home and right to bed. He took all kinds of
medication and was on three different diets, all of them consisting
chiefly of milk. I kept needling him that he ought to have fun and
throw the damn prescriptions out the window. To prove it, I would
mix drinks for myself—remember the Bloody Mary?—consisting
of gin, ketchup, cigar ash, and almost anything that happened to

be handy. I never became ill. Eddie would have some graham crackers and milk and wake up with a bellyache.

When I returned home one night following another late-night round of the speaks, a telegram was under my door at the St. Regis:

I am at the Park Lane. Call me.

It was signed, simply, "N."

I had no idea who "N" might be, as it was almost a year since I had heard from Norma. Hollywood gossip mills had it that she and Roland had just returned from Europe and would be married soon. I thought the wire might be from Pola Negri, wishing to rekindle the affair we had had very briefly a few months before. I called the Park Lane and was told that Miss Negri was not registered. "But," said the operator, when she learned who I was, "we do have a big thrill here at the hotel. Norma Talmadge is with us!"

"Put me through," I told her. Norma and I had a casual chat, and she asked me to lunch with her the next day. As I had a matinee, I told her it would have to be an early lunch, and we agreed, instead, on a late breakfast.

That hour or so I spent with Norma was a very strange one. She seemed tired, perhaps even bored, and the conversation lagged, and then quit completely. We said goodbye and left each other—ice cold, just a handshake. I stepped into a friendly neighborhood speakeasy I knew and had a big hooker of whiskey. The bartender was surprised. "I thought you didn't drink until after the show, Mr. Jessel."

"I usually don't, but something just died."

We then had a drink together.

A few nights later, Norma came to the theater with a party. Cantor and I had the house lights turned on, and I introduced her to the audience. Following the show, she came backstage looking radiantly beautiful. "The show is excellent," she greeted me. "Won't you join me and my friends for supper at the Central Park Casino?"

I told her I would come as soon as I was dressed. Following our last meeting, I was cool and a bit hesitant. At the Casino, we talked as if we had just met for the first time. Finally, I suggested that we would find a warmer atmosphere at a place called the Five O'Clock Club run by some Broadway friends of mine.

"Good. Take me there."

Norma wasn't drinking and I didn't feel like it. To the dismay of the waiter we sat there for three hours with one bottle of Vichy water between us, gazing into each other's eyes like a couple of moonstruck kids. She and Gilbert, she admitted, were going to call it a day. "I have been thinking about you constantly for the past six months, and that is the real reason for my decision."

I told Norma I had never stopped thinking about her since the day of my icy swim in Long Island Sound. When we finally left the Five O'Clock Club, we walked as the cold dawn came up Fifth Avenue as if holding the sleeping moon in her arms.

That night—or dawn—marked the end of my chasing around with girls for a full ten years; well, nearly. (But that doesn't mean the book will be dull from here on in, either.) The next two weeks were wonderful. I spent every waking minute away from the theater with Norma. After seeing her home around one or two each morning—a reasonably early hour for me—I would return to my apartment where Florence's only reaction was, "I hope you're not ill."

Suddenly, Norma was called to the coast on business, but we planned to meet again as soon as possible. She informed me that she intended to retire from the screen and spend the rest of the winter in Palm Beach. Somehow, I would have to figure out a way to join her there. Meanwhile, there was a continuous exchange of telegrams between us as Norma rode the 20th Century Limited and the Santa Fe Chief to Pasadena.

When she arrived on the coast, there was no word from her for two or three days. I began to be a little nervous and wired her, "Tomorrow and tomorrow. . . ."

She telephoned me immediately and said she would soon be leaving for Palm Beach. She added that she loved me more than anything in the world and couldn't wait to see me.

The Cantor-Jessel show left the Palace to play Convention Hall in Cleveland and the Chicago Theater in Chicago. Closing night, I dashed for the train to Palm Beach, still in my makeup, with Milford bringing up the rear and the luggage.

This was to be the most romantic time of my life, and if ever a man was riding on a cloud, it was me when Norma arrived. I held her hand tightly, we looked into each other's eyes for a moment as we stood on the platform. A voice inside me said: "Kid, hold this moment. Don't ever let it go."

I had intended to spend two weeks in Palm Beach. I stayed only ten days. But those 240 hours were the closest I will ever come to heaven, I am sure. Norma was the guest of the former Fifth Avenue modiste, Madame Frances (Mrs. Nathan Spingold). We would spend the mornings and afternoons beside the Spingold pool and at sundown go out for cocktails before adjourning to someone's house for dinner, where Norma was usually the guest of honor.

On the ninth day, I received a telephone call from New York. It was a request for me to return to pinch hit for Cantor on the Chase and Sanborn hour. I was loath to leave, but I was told that my appearance might result in a very long engagement.

I took the last possible train from Palm Beach, and when I arrived at Penn Station, my attorney, Ted Lesser, met me with the bad news. The New York columnists, Lyons, Winchell, all of them, had been printing items steadily about Norma and our romantic idyll in Palm Beach. There had also been many pictures in the papers and magazines at dinner parties. Florence, said Ted, had been raising hell for the first time. She had never paid any attention to any of my romantic escapades or well-publicized affairs, but this time she deduced it was serious. Lesser doubted that she would divorce me, but added he felt that she was in a mood to sue Norma for alienation of affection.

If Florence did decide to divorce me, it would call for such a large settlement that I would be unable to pay it. Even though I was earning a great deal of money, I was still paying off the government for back taxes and for my production failures. Besides, my tremendous family obligations, my mother and cousins, kept me constantly short of cash. With this depressing news, I had to go directly to the radio conference. I was worried to death that Florence might bring suit against Norma and drag her name through the courts and the newspapers.

When I arrived at the offices of the advertising agency, I found myself with a group of men completely alien to my theatrical world. They talked about what I was to do as a substitute for Eddie. I was not to attempt to be funny. I was there as a sort of goodwill "keeper of the bees," so to speak, until Eddie returned. I was to tell no jokes in dialect, and under no circumstances was I to sing. The client disliked my style of singing. The client's aunt, it turned out, a lady well on in years, had once heard me sing a song in Hebrew and Russian and wouldn't dream of having anything like that on her nephew's program. It was no use trying to explain to these advertising idiots—and they still strangle and dictate to the television business even today—that I had been singing in English since I was six years old.

With my mind on my other troubles, I agreed to everything. When one of the clowns said that I would start the following Sunday, I muttered, "I can't believe that Florence will sue Norma."

They looked at me in amazement; I grabbed someone else's hat and rushed out of the office. I had quite a session with Florence and she was unnaturally calm. She had become a full-fledged Christian Science practitioner, and her only hope was that I had not fallen too deeply into Error to be saved. She declared that she would make no move of any kind, that she had no thought of divorcing me. "Your conduct will be the deciding factor, George!"

Her attitude was that she was my wife and had lived up to the marriage contract even if I hadn't. She tried to make the point that, even though I had spread the word that she thought about nothing but Christian Science, she had never refused to share my bed. Apparently Florence had forgotten that two years before she had told me in no uncertain terms that, if I ever wished to "cohabit" with her, I should please let her know early in the evening so that she could be "prepared!" That was a switch. When we were going together, and after we were first married, she would cohabit anywhere—the back of a taxicab, in a Central Park hansom cab, anywhere. I would be damned before I would make an appointment to "cohabit" with my wife.

Also, Florence's practicing was starting to take its toll upon my psyche and temper as well. One early morning when I arrived home about 3:00 A.M., and half-stewed, the telephone was ringing.

It was an actor-vaudevillian I had known for years, Herman Timberg, then on in years. He asked if he could speak to Florence. When I told him she was asleep he asked me to help him.

"George, I've had terrible headaches for two days now, and Florence told me if I read page eighty of the *Science and Health* book, they would go away. Well, I've read it three or four times now and I've still got the headaches."

By this time, in my half-stewed condition, I was ready to throw the telephone at him.

"Well, Herm, I'll tell you what,. why don't you just read it again, and if that doesn't work, why don't you shove the book up your ass and maybe that will."

I don't think Herm ever told Florence about our conversation.

Anyway, I could not feel sorry for her because she, herself, had told me many times that the only thing that was important to her was her religion. My first thought was of Norma. I telephoned her and she started for New York.

My shows for Chase and Sanborn were awful because of the strangling (to a performer) restrictions they had placed upon me. Even my dear mother, Charlotte, who thought my sneezing was more melodious than the violin of Kreisler, ducked the issue when I asked her how she liked the program. All I did was count the hours until Norma would be with me once again. For the first time, my career as a performer was forgotten completely.

Norma arrived, bronzed by the Florida sunshine, and I told her of my troubles with Florence. She decided to telephone Joe in California and have him, as an old friend, and one formerly engaged to Florence, to use his influence so that there would be no legal problems or newspaper headlines. He also advised Norma to go to Europe; the trip would be good for her.

When Joe did call Florence and told her that Norma was going abroad, she was pacified. This was due partly to the fact that she knew I had signed a radio contract and would have to stay. But I didn't.

My programs became less and less entertaining, and a couple of weeks later, I resigned and sailed for Europe. Seven days later, I leaped off the Cherbourg-to-Paris boat train, and Jack Curtis, an old friend I had cabled, was waiting for me in the little bar of the Gare St. Lazare. He gave me the message that Norma was waiting for me at a party. I told my valet Monroe to take my things to the Georges V where I had cabled for reservations. I rushed to Norma's side.

We stayed on in Paris for a few days and then motored south to the Riviera. Each day was happier than the one before, each night more perfect. Then the news came from New York in the form of a cable from Lesser. Winchell had gotten word of our European jaunt, and there were definite divorce rumors. I decided to ask Ted to make Florence a sensible offer of alimony; Norma and I would separate for a while, but nothing could keep us apart eventually.

I returned to New York on the *Leviathan* while Norma stayed behind in Paris. We talked almost hourly on the ship-to-shore radio telephone. When a connection was impossible, I would walk around the deck by the hour. I made up my mind it would be best not to see Norma again until everything could be straightened out, even if it took months. I promised myself I would get her on the telephone and tell her so, but I didn't. I returned to Paris on the *Bremen* the next day. Monroe was having fits trying to keep my clothes pressed.

I stayed in Paris for two days, and Norma came back to New York with me. Florence granted the divorce. The settlement, including attorneys' fees, came to over $150,000. I didn't have the money, but Norma loaned me $100,000 of it. But she did even more than that: She made it possible for me to pay her back by appearing on the stage with me. We did five and six shows a day, yet all she took for her salary was expenses for herself and her maid and secretary. The theaters paid us more than $10,000 per week. Eventually, Norma was tired out from appearing on the stage and returned to California for a rest. I stayed on in New York to take another crack at radio, flying out to the coast almost every week on the American Airlines *Mercury* to Grand Central Air Terminal in Glendale. Norma had not yet discussed a divorce with Joe.

I then made an eight-week tour with Eddie, playing one-night stands. With the great deal of money I earned from this tour and the occasional nightclub shot, which I loathed, I saved enough to buy a house in Palm Beach, which I gave Norma as a gift. While she stayed in the house, I joined Cantor for a tour of the south and chartered a plane so I could fly back each night. There was no landing field in Palm Beach, but Norma would arrive at the scheduled time at an open field in West Palm Beach, flash the head-lights of her Rolls-Royce, and have the chauffeur build a small fire to guide the pilot to the landing spot.

The Cantor-Jessel circus closed its tour in Miami playing the Olympia Theater for two nights—on closing night, there was an as-sassination attempt on the life of newly elected President Franklin Delano Roosevelt by Guiseppe Zangara. The show closed early that night.

Nevertheless, I was at peace with the world.

11

Norma and I Are Married

Norma was called back to California because of the illness of her mother. We both knew, before she left, that the hour had arrived for her to start divorce proceedings against Joe now that my problems with Florence had been resolved.

I returned to New York and began an engagement in a revue called *Casino Varieties* with the Ritz Brothers, the De Marcos, Gertrude Niesen, and Walter O'Keefe. The show had been hooked up so expensively with that cast and such high production values that the management had to lose money even if the theater was SRO at every performance. I was personally successful with an imitation of Chaplin and the Professor Larbermarcher routine.

The night the show closed, Norma returned to New York, but she had spent a day in Mexico on the way and divorced Joe—very amicably as it turned out. We planned to be married immediately and decided that some little town in New Jersey would cut down the chances of a circus atmosphere. Nucky Johnson, then political boss of Atlantic City, for whom I had often performed at his many benefits for the underpriviledged (most of them registered voters), called me and said he would arrange everything after he had heard

110

of our plans. We would be married in his apartment by the mayor of Atlantic City, Harry Bachrach. Norma, I, Milford, and one of his many wives, started for Atlantic City in a second-hand limousine I had purchased from a guy on Broadway. The car broke down and we had to take taxis from Trenton to Atlantic City.

The six years that followed were the happiest any two people, in real life or romantic fiction, could have known. That this marriage, in the end, could be wrecked by a vindictive secretary was unthinkable to us and the people who knew us well. That we two should be as one for the rest of our lives had been the thought that had passed through Norma's mind many years before—on that cold day I took a swim off Harris's dock on Long Island. She finally told me this one warm evening in Palm Beach when I asked her to walk in my garden so that my roses could see her.

Nothing, we thought that night, would ever separate us; the flowers we had placed on the tomb of Abelard and Heloise at the Père Lachaise cemetery in Paris, would never fade; each day and night would bring us closer together. Now, the only thing for me to do was to work my head off and keep the money rolling in. Every man has one great love in his lifetime; Norma was mine.

Naturally, Norma had a great deal of money, and I was in no position to keep her in the manner to which she was accustomed. I did the best I could trying to arrange my appearances so that I could spend most of my time with her. She liked to spend the summers in California and the winters in Florida. This was awfully tough for me. Only in motion pictures or radio (in those days) could you take time off for summer vacations, certainly not winters. Broadcasts could be made from almost anywhere, but you couldn't be in a play, a revue, or what have you, or tour the country, and stop at the height of the season.

I decided, therefore, to get into radio or motion pictures (again) and give up the stage entirely. Radio in those days was a wonderful thing. It changed our lives as much as television did two decades later. I decided to try my hand at it, in spite of the disaster I had had while I was courting Norma and subbing for Eddie. The big problem with the latter was that I was so restricted in what I could and could not do that I could not be myself. The geniuses of Madison Avenue saw to that.

George Burns was sensationally successful by this time and was fairly leaping with radio ideas. It was my turn, now, to ask him for advice. I gritted my teeth and started to work with George and Sam Carlton with an idea Sam had developed, "Amateur Night on the Air." I would put on people from all walks of life, and the amateur receiving the most applause would continue with the show for thirteen weeks. This was two years or so before Major Bowes and, eventually, Ted Mack made a lifetime career of such a program, with Mack even carrying it through to television.

I auditioned the show for an advertising agency with the hope they might use it for a cigarette account I knew was looking for a show. Their attitude was, "We are surprised, Mr. Jessel, with your background, you would even consider a radio audience listening to amateurs."

I gave up the idea, fast. They hired some spiritual singers instead and that show was cancelled within six weeks.

As usual, I needed money and talked some booking agents into a few one-week spots around the country, Columbus, Baltimore, Pittsburgh, and towns north, east, south, and west. I never got less than $5,000 or $6,000 for these engagements, and I again had a few bucks in my pocket. It was a rough way to make a living, not to mention the pain of being separated from Norma. My telephone bills to the coast and to Florida were taking a good chunk of my salary. I decided to fly to the coast and spend some time with my bride.

Norma's beach house at Santa Monica—later occupied by Cary Grant while he and Barbara Hutton were married—was right on the ocean. Norma loved pets around the house, including Topsy, a miserable little Peke, and a parrot. I am sure that damn parrot once resided in a brothel before being acquired by Norma. As soon as there was company in the house, the bird would shriek at the top of its lungs: "Mrs. Edwards, Minnie, Jennie, Annie. Hurry down. Company in the parlor. Company in the parlor!" The damn bird would laugh mockingly at anything I said. He didn't care for me, but he loved Norma, though, and at night before she covered him, she would say, very softly, "Good night, boy!" He would almost croon, "Good night, mother!"

When I tried to get on his good side by uncovering him in the morning, he would look at me and yell, "Go to the office, go to the office!" We never did get along.

While in Santa Monica, I received a telegram telling me, via Sam Carlton, that CBS would engage me for a sustaining program with the hope they could sell me (like a pound of potatoes) to a sponsor. My spirits rose again, and I returned to New York to prepare for it. A week later I began the show, but they were unable to sell it. Nevertheless, it lasted for the full cycle of thirteen weeks while Norma lived at the Palm Beach house I had given her. I would fly down immediately after each show and come back in time for the next one. Three days of basking in the Florida sunshine added up to the happiest home atmosphere imaginable.

However, the contrast between living like a bloated coupon clipper and being on a sustaining radio show was like the difference between baked alaska and cold beans. The radio show was going nowhere and no sponsor would have me at any price. CBS was looking for an out for the second thirteen-week option and I gave them one.

One night, while introducing a tenor, I said, "Ladies and gentlemen, the next singer is a young man with a lovely tenor voice. When I was a boy I sang soprano, and my voice stayed high for so long my parents were frightened." The next day I was told by CBS that the joke was in very bad taste and the show was cancelled forthwith.

By this time it was April and the Palm Beach season was nearly over. Norma and I stayed until the first of June. Visiting us were Norma's two little nephews, Bobby and Jimmy, her sister Natalie's children by Buster Keaton. One night about 7:00 P.M., Max Baer, then the heavyweight champion, telephoned. He was calling from Daytona, where he had refereed a match, and was driving to Miami, but it would be quite late before he got there. He wanted to know if he could spend the night with us and save that extra hundred miles or thereabouts.

"Is there room for a girl friend, too?" he inquired, when Norma said it was fine.

"Of course," said Norma.

"Okay, I'll call her and she should be there in a few minutes. She's in Palm Beach now."

In a little while, a very lovely young thing arrived at the house. As soon as Bobby and Jimmy were told that the heavyweight champ would soon be there to join the young lady, they jumped for joy and begged to be allowed to stay up and meet Max.

"Of course," replied Aunt Norma. "But if it's too late, you must wait until morning."

At eleven we were still waiting. The boys were sent to bed. At one o'clock, big, jovial, happy Max lumbered in. His reason for being late, he explained, was that he had stopped off for a few drinks with friends on the way. I suggested a drink and handed him the bottle, knowing his capacity. Max and his girl sat down on a big Mizner armchair. One arm was around the girl, softly stroking one of her rather ample boobs, and his free hand was on the whiskey bottle. I won't mention where one of her hands was reposing. After all, Norma and I were very broadminded and the kids had been sent to bed. Or so we thought.

Hearing the commotion, they had tiptoed downstairs, and before we could warn Max, they rushed over to him. "Oh, Mr. Baer, are you really the champion?" they asked almost in unison.

"That's right, kids," replied Max, without missing a stroke. His girl friend did.

"How did you come to be such a great fighter?" asked Jimmy.

"Clean living," replied Max, without hesitation.

We sent the kids back to bed, but not before Max promised to swim with them the next day. He was good to his word.

A few days later we all went back to New York and then out to the coast on the Broadway Limited and the Santa Fe Chief. Norma hated to fly. I felt I would try pictures again. I started reading stories and books hoping to get something to produce or write for the screen. In the meantime, Norma had built a tremendous estate just off Benedict Canyon, six minutes from Beverly Hills by car. It seemed like a ranch in those days of sparse population. Far off in the mountains, deer used to drink at the pool every morning. Norma had also taken great pains to make my suite comfortable. I had a workroom, a bedroom, a bath, and a tremendous sun porch. All I needed now was a job.

I ran across a book called *God's Angry Man*, a virile, moving account of the life of John Brown. What a picture this would make,

My dear mother just before her death.

(Above) A wedding picture with my first, Florence Courtney. (1920) (Below) Norma Talmadge and I at our wedding in Atlantic City.

Studio portrait with Norma in 1932. (Photo: Maurice Seymour)

(Left) A picture of my thi
wife, Lois Andrews, i
scribed, "Darling, may v
always be inseparabl
(Photo: Bruno of Hollywo
(Below) With my daugh
Jerilynn, then sixtee
and now a schoolteach
in Kansas. Her moth
was Lois Andrews. (Ph
Le Baron Studios)

(Above) Joan Tyler, the mother of Chrissie. A really beautiful woman. (1959)
(Below) My daughter Chrysa, Chrissie, age eight.

With Rita Hayworth at Ciro's on the night of our aborted wedding trip to Las Vegas.

(Above) With Vivien Leigh at a party at the Savoy Hotel in London in 1964, three years before her death at the age of fifty-three. (Whitestone Photo) (Below) With another love, Abigail "Tommy" Adams, who committed suicide because she couldn't make it in Hollywood.

(Top left) With one of my favorite people, Marlene Dietrich. (Top right) With Alfred G. Vanderbilt, Jr., with whom I played charity softball games in Miami Beach, and Virginia Bruce. Universal Studios, 1937. (Photo: Herbert Dallinger) (Bottom left) Arriving in Paris with Zsa Zsa Gabor. (Bottom right) With Christine Jorgensen, the original sex change celebrity. I'm just trying to see if they're genuine.

I felt, with the right star. I knew just the man: John Barrymore, by then a little too old and dissipated to play a gallant lover or a swashbuckling hero. But Jack was nowhere to be found. He had disappeared after a quarrel with his latest wife. I finally managed to locate Lionel, who told me Jack was at his hillside castle and that he would phone and arrange for an appointment.

I met Jack on the patio and I explained the book to him and said that I would like him to agree to do the film. But before he would even discuss it, he ordered a pitcher of martinis (at 10:00 A.M., mind you) and promptly proceeded to drink from the jug rather than the glass. I started to act out the book for him—ham that I was—and then he joined in at the top of his voice.

Several times during my dissertation, so wrapped up in the book was he, that he promptly proceeded to pee right where he sat. It was disconcerting, to say the least, as I had on $75 alligator shoes and it splashed all over them when it hit the cement.

Nevertheless, I left Barrymore with his agreement to do the picture provided I could come up with the necessary financing and salary for him. That night, at the Trocadero, he again assured me it was all right to go ahead and make the arrangements. I took him at his word, having no experience at dealing with Jack when he was sober, let alone drunk.

The following morning I was in the office of Jesse Lasky, who had a releasing contract for one film. Because he had no suitable property at the time, he would let me use his release if I could bank the contract. Over the telephone from Jesse's office, I made an appointment with J. Cheever Cowdin, president of Universal, and flew to New York to tell him of my plans. Cowdin had long since forgiven me about the Brice and Lillie episode with Rogers. He headed the company at the time and Rogers had related our conversation to him.

Cowdin was interested, but he doubted whether I could deliver Barrymore. "These newspaper stories are so exaggerated," I explained. "If Jack lights a cigarette, the papers say he is trying to start a forest fire. If he drinks a glass of beer, they say he passed out. No, no, Mr. Cowdin, Barrymore is really enthusiastic about the project. He loves the character. To prove it, let me call him if I may be permitted to use your telephone. . . ."

"Surely," replied Cowdin, handing me the instrument, "but I think you'll be disappointed. I know John Barrymore."

As soon as I had Jack on the telephone I knew there was trouble. He shouted that he had no idea what I was talking about and didn't even remember meeting me, let alone peeing all over my alligator shoes. "You can go to hell," were his final words.

There was nothing I could do after that. I apologized to Cowdin. But I must add here that, following that incident, I spent many happy hours with Jack until he died. His closest pal, artist John Decker, even insisted on painting a portrait of me as the Immortal Bard. The portrait, now very valuable because of the artist, still hangs in my Encino living room.

Jack admitted he knew the book, wanted to do the picture, but could never recall our conversation on his patio or at the Trocadero; nor could he recall our conversation on the telephone from Cowdin's office. He was so drunk, I assumed, he lost all contact with reality over this and many other matters. He had gotten to the point, I learned later, that he could hardly remember anything from one hour to the next.

Back in Hollywood again, I was ashamed of my failure. I wasn't quite so sweet around the house, either. Norma and I weren't as close as we had been. Now what to do? I started reading American history as an escape. In an obscure passage of one book, I discovered the name of Haym Solomon. I set out to learn all I could about this man. With the exception of Thomas Paine, no other American patriot has been so completely ignored. Solomon had been imprisoned by the British at the start of the American Revolution. While awaiting execution, he escaped. He then made fortunes in commerce and gave everything he could beg, borrow, or steal from the British, to Washington and his Forces of Independence. Haym Solomon's story has never been completely told in America.

This was a role for Paul Muni who was under contract to Warner Brothers. While Jack and I were not socializing, we remained on friendly terms in spite of *The Jazz Singer* fiasco. I called him, told him about Solomon, and he hired me over the telephone to do some additional research and write a treatment. Nothing much came of it except a two-reel short.

When it was finished, Jack asked me to remain on the payroll as assistant to Mervyn Le Roy, his brother-in-law.

Mervyn had great respect for me as a showman, as we had met and talked many times. He was tired of "yes men," he told me, and wanted honest opinions on everything. He was planning a film called *Fools for Scandal,* an original story to star the French heartthrob Fernand Gravet and Carole Lombard.

When I read it, I told him it was an adaptation from an old Hungarian farce and that I didn't like it at all and felt it would make a lousy picture. Apparently, my opinion wasn't worth much and a short time later I was dismissed. Although Mervyn produced and directed many great and successful motion pictures following *Fools for Scandal,* this one was a miserable failure.

I am not referring to Mervyn when I say the following, but I feel it is as good a time as any to bring out the fact that "mediocrity" in the lower echelons is what has been wrong with the motion picture, radio, and television industries for years. Those at the top only want mediocrity below them because they are so insecure themselves they feel that, if they hire anyone with talent, they, themselves, will soon be out of a job.

But it was I who was out of a job at this particular time, which meant back to radio or Broadway once more. Norma was losing confidence in me, or something. She even ventured to suggest that all these dismissals must be my fault; the whole picture business couldn't be wrong.

I was beginning to agree with her.

12

Trouble in My Marriage

Two days later, ever reliable Sam Carlton called me from New York to tell me that Ben Rock, the radio impresario, had a marvelous idea for me to return to radio—a cooperative venture with as many sponsors as there were stations. The idea was to interpolate a minute's pause at the beginning, in the middle, and at the end of a program. Then the various stations would cut in with their own local commercials.

The Mutual Network agreed to give us blanket network coverage, and no sponsor or advertising agency would have any say about the actual format of the show or program content. We planned to begin modestly with three sponsors, one in New York and two in California.

Norma agreed to come on the show with me, not only to help me, but to give her something to do. In fact, almost every star in Hollywood who wasn't under contract agreed to cooperate without compensation to keep their names before the public. This included such a lineup as Eddie Cantor, Penny Singleton, Weber and Fields, Judy Garland, Burt Wheeler, Glenda Farrell, Bobby Breen, Buck Jones, Irving Berlin, and so on down the list. Soon, because of this lineup of ''names,'' we had twenty additional sponsors and the program was going well.

I managed to hit the front page of nearly every newspaper by attacking the radio, film, and gossip commentators headed, at the time, by Jimmy Fidler.

''What right,'' I asked the radio audience, ''did a hair tonic or soap company have to present a man on the air to sing the praises of their product, asking the public to buy it, and then knock another man's product—a motion picture?

''If,'' I continued, ''a soap company employee can tell the public not to see a certain picture 'because it is so bad,' then who is to stop me from saying, '20th Century-Fox has a great film, be sure to see it, but please don't use so and so's soap because it is bad for your skin'.''

This didn't endear me to Madison Avenue or the commentators, but I thought it honest and constructive criticism. I also thought it would endear me to the film producers. They did rally 'round me, writing me letters of appreciation, but with never an offer of a picture deal. Fidler, George Fisher, and the others did not debate the subject. But listeners, from then on, very seldom heard a scathing film review from their ilk. If the commentators didn't like a picture, they just didn't review it on the air, period.

On the show I introduced a new band out of Chicago, Tommy Tucker, which went on to fame and fortune in the ''big band'' era, and I gave Frances Gumm the name of Judy Garland. Later, Norma and the entire troupe played and broadcast from key cities all over the country. But, unfortunately, the cooperative radio idea didn't work out for obvious reasons. A station or sponsor in Cleveland who paid only $35 a week for the show, didn't like the band; the maiden aunt of another sponsor in Chicago who paid $200 didn't like me, and so on. We could get no renewals for the following year, despite the fact that the listeners had shown their approval of the show by mail, and the theaters in which we broadcast the show were always packed.

At the end of the last show, I received a call from columnist Leonard Lyons saying that President Roosevelt wished to see me as he wanted a few laughs. I needed a few myself. Over the years I often visited FDR, and he was also very friendly with Lenny, one of the best Broadway columnists of all times to my way of thinking. Every time FDR wanted to see me, he would have his secretary Marvin McIntyre telephone Lenny and ask him to find me and summon me to the Oval Office as soon as I could get free. At the time, FDR was having trouble with Congress, Hitler was kicking up his heels against the Czechs and Austrians, and he was feeling down in the dumps.

Just as I arrived in the Oval Office and sat down on the couch, Marvin walked in. "I know you're about to have a few laughs with Mr. Jessel, Mr. President, but Henry Ford, Sr., is downstairs and would like to pay his respects."

FDR looked at me, and through his famous grin, said, "George, if you ever repeat what I'm going to say I'll have you deported to Russia." Then he turned to Marvin and, in deadly earnest, said, "Marvin, tell Henry Ford that I said he can go and fuck himself!"

FDR then explained that he had no time for any American industrialist or public figure who had allowed himself to be presented with a decoration by Adolf Hilter. Until now, I have never repeated this story except to the Ford family after the Senior Ford's death. I have always been very friendly with the entire family.

(Before he died, Ford deeply regretted accepting a medal from Hitler and realized he had been made a tool for Goebbels's propaganda machine.)

Another reason the president had sent for me at this particular time was to ask me to preside at a dinner for the Russian ambassador, Maxim Litvinoff, who was returning to Russia. I suddenly recalled the conversation I had had with the little tailor from Seattle in that delicatessen with Jolson and Cantor so many years before. In my mind, I cooked up a little surprise for the ambassador. I never mentioned it beforehand to FDR, but my listening to that little man provided me with the biggest laugh of the evening in an otherwise very dull proceeding. I used it to open my remarks:

"Mr. President, Mr. Ambassador, ladies and gentlemen. Men in their later years, under the stress of circumstances and amidst the glory of their success and the sunshine brilliance of their fame, often revert to their early beginnings, the sweet and simple incidents of their early years, their innocent childhood. So I know that if our guest of honor this evening could give us one message, he would say, 'For good cleaning and dyeing see my brother, Morris Finkelstein, on Turk Street in San Francisco. . . .'"

It brought a loud laugh from the ambassador, a huge grin from the president, and a nervous laugh, to start, from the black-tie audience until they saw the mirthful reaction of Litvinoff. It loosened up the proceedings considerably.

But unfortunately, Litvinoff quickly disappeared after returning to Moscow because he favored *detente* with the U.S. Some friends told me many years later that he died of quick pneumonia—bullets in the lungs—which often happens in Utopia. But, in a private conversation with the ambassador—when I had requested his permission to use the anecdote about his brother—I discovered he had fine feelings for his adopted country and did not believe, even though he had left it to take up with the Communists, in the vicious speeches then being made by the then Red leaders against the United States.

Two or three years later, FDR again summoned me to the Oval Office to make a presentation to Sir Alexander Fleming, the discoverer of the wonder drug penicillin. Secretary of State Cordell Hull was supposed to present the citation to Sir Alex but was indisposed.

After I had made a short speech extolling the virtues of penicillin, I whispered to Sir Alex, "I know it's a wonderful discovery, sir, but I can't take it. I break out with the smallest dose."

Sir Alex laughed and whispered back, "Neither can I. It does the same thing to me!"

Following the collapse of the show and my visit with FDR, I was asked to rush back to Hollywood as general advisor for a tremendous radio show—the Maxwell House Coffee Hour—done in cooperation with Metro-Goldwyn-Mayer and all their stars. This program had been on the air for two or three weeks and it had suffered as entertainment from too much technical know-how, as well as being overproduced and over-rehearsed. That was MGM's way.

I conferred with Louis K. Sidney, who was in charge, and suggested that MGM only use those performers who had specialties to offer. I insisted, for instance, that Fannie Brice use her "Baby Snooks" routine and that Judy Garland sing songs that the public were already singing and whistling, not slick, new MGM musical numbers written for a show that the radio audience had never heard before.

One of the account executives did not like Judy—for what reason we won't go into here (she was underage at the time)—and I incurred his wrath when I questioned his judgment. After all, he was from the high and mighty advertising world of Madison Avenue and knew it all.

The program became quite a success, thanks to my suggestions, which, this time, were all followed. As a result, after a month of this, my services were no longer needed. I had doctored the show, but they kept me on the payroll—at a very good salary—for three more months and then I left with no ill feelings. I felt I had accomplished something in radio. Nevertheless, it again upset Norma that I was no longer on a permanent basis with someone or other.

She suggested we take a vacation in Honolulu. I told her it was too far away from the scene of theatrical and radio activity to enable me to line myself up again, and I suggested a quick trip to Europe. There was a hit play running in London I wanted to take a look at called *Spring Meeting*. I thought I might be able to get it for American production. Also, several months before, Grover Whelan and the committee being formed for the New York World's Fair had asked me to dig up some ideas while I was abroad. A few days in London, a few days in Paris, possibly Rome and Vienna, I told Norma.

She felt that such a trip would be too hurried for her and would mean too much dashing around. She told me I could go if I wished, and I started to notice a little coolness in her tone. A few days later, however, I sailed on the *Queen Mary*, which set the trans-Atlantic speed mark on this particular trip. While I was involved in a heavy stakes bridge game, the overseas operator sent for me. Would I come to his office on the bridge, as London was calling me.

A very British voice came over the static. "Mr. Jessel, we understand the *Queen* is in the middle of a record-breaking voyage. The *Daily Mail* would like a few words from you on how it feels to be traveling so fast."

I could not believe that a London newspaper such as the *Daily Mail* would be interested in what I had to say about such a feat. Earlier that same day I had been heckled quite loudly by another Englishman while I was acting as the auctioneer for the daily distance pool. Because he had been nipping rather heavily, I ignored him, but the thought crossed my mind that this might be a hoax by him. It sounded a great deal like him:

"Listen, kid," I replied, "I am in the middle of a high stakes bridge game. Don't make any jokes with me. I've just bid five clubs, and if I lose, I'll sue you."

About twenty minutes later, I was called out of another hand and again told that London was calling. This time, said the operator, it was the *Daily Express.* I made up my mind to put an end to what I still thought was a hoax by the imbibing Englishman, as well as giving the operator a little hell. "I know you want me to tell you how it feels to be on a record-breaking ocean liner. Why don't you ask the captain, if he isn't sleeping? All the other officers are drunk, and you, my friend, are a crashing bore. If you call me out of my bridge game again, I'll see that the bartender serves you a Mickey at dinner."

The radio operator rushed out of his booth just as I hung up. Excitedly, he told me that the London newspapers *were* actually calling me, and he feared the consequences for Cunard of what I'd said. He called back and tried to square things away and did, to a measure, explaining my feelings and the reason for them.

When I arrived at Southampton, the *Express* announced: "George Jessel refused to talk about the crossing. This is the novelty of the London theatrical season. . . ."

I spent three days in London, lonely for Norma and worried about her coolness, but I was consoled by the wonderful company of George M. Cohan who crossed to London with me. The last night before leaving for Paris on the *Golden Arrow,* I called Norma in California. I missed her so much that I promised to return on the first boat from Cherbourg after a day or two in Paris. It turned out to be the *Normandie,* making one of her last voyages before she burned and turned turtle at her New York pier.

Norma agreed to come to New York and meet me. When I arrived at the St. Regis, I found her with a bad cold from the train trip. I also found her even cooler than she had been before I left. Her maid advised me that she was "starting her menopause and is very nervous, Mr. Jessel."

I had to remain in New York for a series of meetings with Whelan and the World's Fair Committee so I sent Norma to Palm Beach. I suggested to Whelan that they build a replica of "Little Old New York," having the Fair design and build the attraction with myself having a small share of the profits—the whole thing to be operated under my name and direction. It would cost half a million, according to Whelan's estimates. (I could have done it all for less than $300,000.)

After that was settled, I joined Norma for a holiday. She was still quite ill and very nervous, and the stabbing thought started to hit me that she didn't love me anymore. My presence seemed to make her more nervous than ever. The skies cleared; she got a little better. One night we walked along the beach together as we had so many times in the past. I took her in my arms and held her. She was silent, but that silence bespoke a thousand words to me, and the lyrics of "The Thrill Is Gone" kept rushing through my mind. We walked silently and then, out of the blue, Norma said, "I had my fortune told and I'm going to fall in love with a tall blond man."

"If it's the same fortune teller who told me last year I would be a millionaire, I'm happy," I replied, stunned. But it was then I knew my marriage to Norma Talmadge was about to collapse in ruins. To take my mind off the situation, I returned to New York to supervise the World's Fair project.

For several years, I had maintained a small office in Hollywood that was looked after by my cousin Dan and a middle-aged secretary. This lady had been with me during most of my motion picture jobs in Hollywood, and she liked working for me because I was very seldom in the office. I telephoned her and told her there was no business in Hollywood for me anymore, particularly with my World's Fair involvement. I then added that I would have to let her go with a month's salary. She was very disappointed that I didn't bring her to New York. As things turned out, I wish now I had.

Norma came to New York, grudgingly I felt, for the opening.

Al Smith and his wife, and an audience of some thirty thousand people attended the opening on a bright, sunlit day. While not a great success financially, it did very well. Billy Rose's Aquacade was directly across the way from us, and we got the overflow who couldn't get in over there.

Norma was ill at ease and very nervous again. She made up her mind to return to California. Constance, her sister, Dr. Blaustein, an old friend, Norma, and I dined at the Oak Room of the Plaza before she left. She kissed me goodbye hurriedly and, as she slammed the door of her compartment, looked me in the eye and stabbed me: "Now you can sleep with every blonde chorus girl in New York!"

I hadn't slept with any blondes in New York or anywhere else. But if she was jealous I felt it was a good sign. It meant, I thought, that she still loved me. I received a rather warm wire from Chicago and another from the coast. She said the house was rather lonely, the Peke had been killed, and the parrot had stopped talking. The following night I telephoned her.

"Hello, darling, how are you feeling?" I inquired in my jauntiest, happily married man tone.

The voice, which had been so warm, was now ice cold.

"Didn't you get Ingle Carpenter's letter?" she inquired. Ingle was her west coast lawyer.

"No," I replied, a little worried.

"Well, you should have. I am divorcing you. . . ."

After a few stunned moments, "Now come on, honey, you can't mean that," I pleaded.

"Yes, I do, and I am not sick or upset or anything. I mean it," and she sounded like she did, too.

After telling her I would take the first plane to the coast, she informed me it wouldn't do any good; she had made up her mind. I sat there in a stupor for nearly five minutes. I called a friend, Jack Raymond, in Los Angeles. Raymond had worked for me on radio and his wife had been Norma's close confidante for years. All he knew was that my former secretary, the nice, middle-aged lady, had been contacting Norma regularly by telephone in New York, Palm Beach, and Los Angeles for weeks. Apparently, she had been regaling Norma with phony tales as to my "conduct" in the office and my "telephone conversations with imaginary females." In Norma's state of mind she would have believed anything. I was sore as hell about this but not terribly disturbed because my conscience was clear and I felt truth would out.

I spent the night walking around Central Park—it was safe to do so in those days—and decided I would take the *Mercury* to Los Angeles the next day.

When I reached the house in Benedict Canyon, Norma was resting in her suite with a doctor—who later turned out to be a quack who had been defrocked by the American Medical Association—and his nurse in attendance. I asked if I could speak to my wife alone. The nurse thought it could be arranged later but I must leave. These were "Dr. James's orders," she explained.

I went downstairs and noticed quite a few changes. The lady masseuse employed by Norma was now her social secretary, and her husband, who had formerly done nothing but pack and care for Norma's clothes, was ordering lunch in an imperious tone as I walked out the door.

That afternoon Norma and I had a brief but, to me, painful meeting. Then Ingle Carpenter arrived. Carpenter was a competent lawyer and a gentleman. With his partners, he had been Norma's lawyer for years. His feeling for us was fatherly, as he explained to me that papers had already been prepared; there was nothing for me to do but sign them. Alone with me for the moment, Ingle said that he didn't think Norma would go through with the divorce. "She is suffering from nervous tension," he advised, "so do or say nothing under the circumstances."

Prior to our marriage, Norma and I had signed a prenuptial agreement that I would have no share in her personal fortune, nor she in mine, if I had any, in case of a divorce or the death of either one while we were married. Since I had given her the house in Palm Beach, there were no other business matters to discuss. I signed the papers on condition that we insert one little change. Norma was to take no divorce action against me for at least six weeks. At the end of that time, she, through Ingle, was to notify me and I would go away and wouldn't hear about it. Also, there was to be no newspaper story given out without my approval. Then, with a handshake, I left.

I packed my things to return on the night flight and sent roses to Norma before I left, writing on the card the words I had used since our first meeting, "Always roses, always love."

I had dinner at the Trocadero, planning to go from there to Burbank to catch my flight at 11:00 P.M. But as I came out on the sidewalk on Sunset Boulevard, I was just in time to hear the news vendor, who had worked the area for years, yelling, "Norma Talmadge to divorce George Jessel." This, mind you, on the front page in larger type than that used by the same paper to announce Hitler's annexation of Czechoslovakia. During the next few weeks I made several flights back and forth to the coast desperately trying to bring about a reconciliation. I refused to believe it was over, since no other man was mentioned or involved. I hadn't reckoned with the quack; Norma had kept it pretty quiet. But more about that later. The secretary and the quack had done their work well.

All this was between another weekly radio show for a hair tonic sponsor that was going very well, and my supervisory job at the fair. It was hard for me to concentrate with my mind on Venice, Paris, Palm Beach, *The Jazz Singer,* and everything else that had to do with Norma. Added to my radio work, I had been appearing at Loew's State in New York, and during one of the performances, I collapsed on stage. Ben Hecht carried me off and I managed to finish the date after a twelve-hour sleep. I listened to all the old bromides from friends: "There are other fish in the stream"; "Go out and meet some other girls, George. You'll get over it."

For the next couple of months I felt like a pastry chef, as I had one tart after another in and out of my apartment at the St. Regis. I suppose I was trying to prove something, but I didn't know what.

Life was only made bearable by spending every waking minute with George M. Cohan. George's personality was so strong he made me forget myself. I wrote several songs, all in the same vein, each one torchier that the last: "Stop Kicking My Heart Around," "Moon Over Yesterday," and "This, Too, Will Pass, Sweetheart," were just a few of the titles. The first was quite popular, but the last two never even reached a song plugger's piano.

I heard nothing from Norma. I had read in Winchell's column, and Parson's, two days in a row that Norma was being seen around in the company of Roland Drew, an actor. I was sure this was no romance. He was definitely interested in someone else.

It wasn't until George M. and I were having a drink one afternoon in the Oak Room that I even learned I had been divorced. Three reporters, from the AP, UP, and INS, came up to our table and told me.

I had no reaction. George answered for me. "Hollywood couldn't have hurt a sweeter guy," he told them.

The New York World's Fair of 1939–1940, while great in Long Island acreage, had many sad touches that detracted from its gaiety. Like life itself, there was no happy medium. Your concession, your show, or your restaurant was either a great success or a great failure. "Little Old New York" was an exception. It did not do well enough to justify the half-million-dollar investment, but it played to tremendous crowds. One of its seven bars was the Knickerbocker, over 125 feet in length. The bar alone did enough business to realize a good profit, but I found out later I did not share in this. But I didn't care much; nothing mattered to me. Every girl suffered by comparison with Norma. The one night a week I spent at the fair was more pleasant than the others because, as a rule, George M. was with me.

One night at the St. Regis, Sam Carlton and I were preparing the next broadcast. George S. Kaufman was with us, as he was to be the guest star. I had been going around with a beautiful woman and we were very fond of each other in a show business, flamboyant fashion. She had told me repeatedly that she was legally separated from her husband.

As George was leaving, an excited bell captain rang through to tell me that madame's husband was looking for me and threatening to kill me on sight. I was advised not to leave my apartment because the husband was bigger than Joe Louis and just as lethal, according to my intelligence. I telephoned a fellow I knew downstairs and asked him to come up and bring the revolver I knew he always carried. About ten minutes later the excitement died down, the bell captain having convinced my opponent I was not "at home." A few minutes later my pistol-packing friend left, leaving the gun with me for "protection."

Then a friend telephoned me from Palm Beach—it had the beginnings of quite a night. "George, I know that you and Norma are divorced, but she just arrived here, opened part of the house, and passed me on the street today with another guy. She didn't seem to know me and I am sure she is in the hands of some terrible people."

I told him I was sorry to hear that but there was nothing I could do about it from New York. I knew my informant was very fond of the sauce and I felt this was one of those times. I walked to the window, opened the blinds, and looked down at a Manhattan covered with heavy snow and more falling. "Well," I said to myself, "what's going to happen next?"

I didn't have long to wait. Another call from Palm Beach, this time collect from an old gentleman who had been our gardener and handyman. It was practically the same story, although with one additional statement that frightened me. "She has some doctor with her who never leaves her alone," said Sol. "I'm worried for Miss Talmadge."

I called the airport and, of course, no planes were taking off because of the weather. I started drinking, and after a pint of bourbon straight from the bottle, my imagination started to run the gamut of emotions. I felt sure Norma was in the clutches of some very bad people after her fortune. Every other scene from melodramas of women in distress passed through my mind. I tried to charter a plane; no dice.

The last man I spoke to said he knew only one pilot stupid enough to fly in this weather—apart from myself. He said he would try to get in touch with him and have him call me. Sam, who was still with me, suggested I go to bed, take a few more belts and call my masseur, Goldie, to relax me.

Goldie came over, gave me a rubdown, and to add insult to injury, started telling me some jokes I had told Berle months before on the coast. The phone rang and a lilting Irish voice announced that he was the pilot crazy enough to take off on a night like this.

"Where are you?" I inquired.

He gave me an address near an airport on Long Island. Taking Goldie and my revolver with me, we were there in less than an hour. Within twenty minutes I had succeeded in pouring enough whiskey down the throat of the pilot and getting him to agree to fly through the storm. He warned me that I would have to be able "to take it," as he had an open plane that would only hold three

people in a crush. The cost of the round trip would be $1,500. If he
got into any trouble with the law I would have to pay all the fines.
By this time I was so far gone with the booze and the excitement I
couldn't have cared less.

"Come on, Goldie. It's worthwhile being born to have lived on
a night like this. You'll remember it all your life," I added. Goldie
never did forget that night.

On the way down, the pilot turned to me and asked me what
was so urgent that I had to fly to Palm Beach in such weather.

"Because some man has my ex-wife in his clutches and I'm
going to kill the son-of-a-bitch," I replied, very dramatically.
"And here's the gun I'm going to use," I said, as I waved the
weapon around.

"Oh no, you're not," he answered and grabbed the pistol and
threw it over the side. "I'm not going to be an accessory to
murder."

"Now what to do?" I thought to myself. Just then our pilot
announced that he was going to put down in Jacksonville for some
gas. As Goldie and I cooled our heels in the old terminal waiting
room, I spied a policeman I knew from the many times I had
stopped at the airport, if it could be called such in those days,
on my way to Palm Beach. I noticed he had a shiny new pistol on
his belt.

"Hi, Rube," I greeted him. "I see you've got a new gun since I
was here last."

"Yeah, a nice new .45 they just issued us."

"Let me take a look at it," I asked him. A diabolical plan was
forming in my whiskey-soaked mind. I told him I would like to take
it over in the light—it was now dawn—and take a good look at it.
Just at that moment, the pilot informed me that we were ready to
take off.

"I'll be there in just a minute," I told him, all the while inch-
ing toward the gate and admiring the weapon in my hands. As we
reached the gate, I looked at Goldie. "Run," I said; we both ran
and climbed into the plane. Rube was yelling some obscenities at
us, but I had my weapon.

About two hours later, aided by a brisk tail wind, we arrived
in Palm Beach. Our former gardener, whom I had the foresight to

telephone from Jacksonville, was there to meet us. We left the pilot asleep in the cockpit. With Goldie walking nervously beside me, we made our way to the house I had given Norma in happier times.

A husky servant I had never seen before met us at the door and barred the way. "What do you want?" he inquired, rather pompously. I told him I wished to see Miss Talmadge.

"She is asleep and is not to be disturbed for several hours," I was informed. "Doctor's orders."

With the residue of the bourbon still in my bloodstream and my pistol in my back pocket, I told him, in true Jimmy Cagney fashion, "Stand aside." Goldie was shaking in the background looking for a way off the grounds.

"Stay where you are," I admonished, "or my man will kill you," pointing over my shoulder at the trembling masseur. Goldie turned pale and blurted, "No, I won't!"

"Yes, he will," I quickly told the butler or whatever the hell he was. I kicked him in the shins and dashed up the stairs, all the while trying to get the damn gun out of my back pocket. I reached the door of what had been our bedroom.

I knocked very loudly on the locked door. Norma answered rather weakly. She had been dreadfully ill, she explained, and I had not known about it. As gently as I could, I said through the door, "Please listen to me, Norma. I know I have no legal right to enter into your life or your affairs. But the only profound affection I have had in my life are my feelings for you. If you are in any trouble, I'll get you out of it even if I have to swing for it."

I was beginning to sound like a character in a Monogram gangster movie, circa 1930. Nevertheless, I was determined to find out what was going on.

Norma again told me to go away, that I had no right to be there, that she was in no danger, and that she would send for the police if I didn't leave immediately. Very quickly, and with the strength of a gorilla, I ripped the telephone wires out of the wall in the hallway beside me. I pleaded with Norma to send out whoever was in the room with her. If he would explain things to me, I would go away. I added, for good measure, how I had risked my life to come to her side. I thought I noticed a little puddle between Goldie's feet.

Norma's reply was an adamant, "Go away . . . now!"

"If that door isn't open by the time I count three, I'll shoot the lock off," I said, trying to figure out which was the right way to shoot the cannon I had in my hand. The door did not open, and I kept my word. Goldie fled down the stairs. I shot at the lock and the door shattered. I found Norma alone, terrified, and her face tortured with pain. She slapped my face, in spite of the smoking pistol, and just at that moment I saw something rustle the drapes and a figure dive through the open window and onto the roof of the first-floor wing.

I dashed to the window, about twenty feet away, and fired the .45 four or five times at the fleeing figure. The next thing I knew I was being questioned by the Palm Beach police with Sam Harris and Arthur Hammerstein in attendance.

"Do you know one of those bullets you fired hit a gardener square in the rump two blocks away, Mr. Jessel?" asked the burliest of the two cops standing over me. "A few inches higher and you could have killed him."

"Hell, I'm a Jewish comedian, not Buffalo Bill," I quipped, still not realizing what I really had done. It turned out that the man in the room with Norma was the defrocked doctor Carvel James, who had been at Norma's bedside in California. He had been treating Norma ever since she started through the change of life and had reportedly gone after several wealthy women patients during his career. He ended up marrying Norma, and when she died, she left him over a million, and two houses, including the Palm Beach place I had given her many years before.

The next thing I knew I was being hustled aboard a train by Sam Harris after he and Arthur had assured Norma I would never come near her again. She, luckily, refused to file charges. Sam and Arthur also posted a bond with the police department. I was told I could forfeit the peace bond in lieu of an appearance. A deal.

On arriving back in New York, the weather was rotten and I wondered how in the hell that Irishman had ever gotten his plane off the ground, let alone get us to Palm Beach. I found out later his name was Douglas "Wrong Way" Corrigan.

Depressed, I made up my mind to end it all. I wrote a very long letter with a finish that should have been between two slices of rye at the Stage Delicatessen. "Thus, I make my exit from this badly written play of life," I wrote, "leaving exactly as I entered, whining and embittered by it all."

I looked at a revolver I had purchased on Broadway that was now lying on the hall table in front of me. I was about to pick it up when Providence sent George M. Cohan through the open door of my suite at the St. Regis. As he entered I told him, very unemotionally, that I saw no reason to continue; I had nothing to make me happy and, worse still, I was no good to anyone. I then showed George the letter. He read it carefully and then laughed uproariously.

"This letter is terrible," he said. "If you feel you want to do away with yourself, that's up to you, kid, but don't leave a crappy letter like this behind. It sounds like it was written by a mug. I wouldn't want anyone to know I had a pal who would say goodbye to the world as badly as this. Christ," he laughed, "this is the worst thing I have ever read. Let's take a walk and see if we can compose a good letter. Then, you can do anything you want."

We both laughed like hell as we walked around Central Park. I forgot about my plan.

13

I Marry Again

AFTER promising Sam Harris and Arthur Hammerstein I would be a good boy and not shoot any more gardeners or defrocked doctors in the ass, I flew to Palm Beach once again (avoiding the Jacksonville airport) for the Christmas holidays. I was the guest of Sam, who had lined up the very lovely Sunny Ingram as my "chaperone" to see that I stayed out of trouble and avoided Norma.

I did attend one dinner party at which Norma was present with James, but they were sitting several tables away. We never looked directly at each other all evening, although I did notice she was looking a lot better.

After I returned to New York, my broadcasts were getting better and I was whole once again. I decided to resume the weekly trips to Palm Beach realizing I could now face the situation with Norma and James sanely and rationally. It was over, period. There was racing, gambling, and Al Jolson, who was great company if he wasn't having sponsor trouble. I had to leave Miami on Monday nights for my Wednesday broadcast, and I generally took the 8:00 P.M. flight. That meant that after my morning swim in the Atlan-

134

tic, I could go to the races, leave Hialeah at five, and make the plane at eight.

One Monday after placing a $100 bet with a bookie, I decided to leave early and stop by the Roney-Plaza for a drink on the way to the airport. At a table near the door sat Tommy Guinan, an old friend and brother of the famed Texas Guinan. Tommy was with an extraordinarily pretty girl in a bright green dress and a smart white turban. He introduced me to Lois Andrews.

Dressed the way she was, as tall as she was, she looked a great deal older than she later turned out to be. I had heard a lot about this young lady. She had been mentioned frequently in all the gossip columns from coast to coast as the number one glamour girl of New York. I figured she had to be in her late twenties.

After a couple of belts with Tommy and Lois, who stared at me the entire time, I had to leave for the airport. When the plane stopped at Atlanta, I bought a late paper and discovered that the $100 bet I had made at the track had come in at a big price, something like eighty to one. I had a chunk of dough coming my way. When a few days passed in New York and no word from the book, I was worried. I had also been thinking of Lois quite frequently. With the idea of giving the bookie a gentle reminder, I decided to kill two birds with one stone.

I wired Tommy Guinan:

> Tell the Andrews girl she is very cute and I don't blame all those guys falling in love with her. If you see our book tell him any time he wants to send me the dough at the St. Regis, it's o.k.

I received the money by Western Union a few hours later.

The next night at dinner, I was introduced to a very tall and beautiful young lady, Elinor Troy. After that meeting we dined together two or three times, and during one of our conversations, I told her of an idea I had for a musical play that I would like to produce if I had the money. Elinor told me that she would try to get it for me. She knew a very rich man (as most tall and beautiful girls in New York always did), a little on in years, who might be interested in backing a good show.

The next day, Dorothy Kilgallen, in her *New York Journal-American* column, wrote that Elinor Troy would get so and so to back my show. At the time, the man mentioned was a very ardent suitor of Lois Andrews. Lois came to New York to find out why Elinor was encroaching on her bank account. At the Central Park Casino we were introduced to each other again, and the following day I took Lois to lunch at Twenty-One.

For the first time since my separation from Norma, I really felt myself again in the company of this gorgeous girl. After lunch I went to the rehearsal of an American Legion broadcast on which I was to appear with George M. Cohan. He and his pals immediately sensed a change in me. I had the kind of enthusiasm for my work that had been missing for over a year and a half.

The next morning I sang in the bathtub and Schwartz, my new valet, said, "You're either in love again or you've gone crazy altogether."

Little did he—or I—know what was to follow. I did have a new interest in life, and the next day I phoned Lois and asked if I could come 'round and see her. I was staggered when I saw her apartment. Consisting of two bedrooms, living room, and kitchen, it was luxurious to say the least. In the center of the living room was one of the largest record players I had ever seen, surrounded by at least 1,000 records. Her closets were packed with clothes, and enough fur coats were draped around chairs and over sofas to keep a Russian regiment warm in Siberia.

When I arrived, Lois was in the middle of lunch, which consisted of a Nutburger covered in sauces and three bottles of Coca-Cola. I had never met such a girl before. She was a grown woman in the body of a little girl. A native of a small town in California, she had lived on and around Broadway for two years after a stint as a cigarette girl for Earl Carroll's Theater in Hollywood.

I had to leave after several hours, as Lois had a dinner date she could not break. That was the last date she had with anyone else but me for quite a while.

Dining at the Stork Club that evening I was a little taken aback when Sonny Kendis's orchestra started playing my song, "Stop Kicking My Heart Around," and then continued to play ditties of mine, some of which I had forgotten. I approached Sonny and asked him the reason for the George Jessel Music Festival.

"That little lady in the corner asked me to play nothing but your music tonight," replied Sonny, "and she tipped me $100, Georgie."

There, in the corner, was Lois with the gentleman who decided against backing my show. Lois's eyes were glued to my table as I sat back down. I was flattered, to say the least.

The following day I had a date to play bridge with Joe Schenck and some boys at his apartment. I picked up Lois and she sat behind Joe's chair and stared at me. Hand after hand Joe and I were doubled and lost a couple of thousand points in a few minutes. I was thinking only of Lois.

Schenck looked at me. "You'd better marry the girl, and don't play cards again until you have."

It was then three-thirty in the afternoon, and Lois decided she wanted to go to Radio City Music Hall. We left the theater seven hours later. I did not remember anything about the film, *Edison, the Man*, because all I was conscious of were two big eyes, framed by a turbanned head, which nestled on my shoulder. She always wore the turban because it made her look much older.

We decided then and there we would see each other every possible minute. There would be no more boyfriends for Lois, no more affairs for me. The newspaper columnists had often mentioned that Lois was only sixteen. I never brought the subject up because I didn't believe it. It was impossible that such a child could have crowded so much into so few years.

Lois wanted to get married, have a home and child. All the tinsel and glamour of Broadway meant nothing to her, she said. I told her I thought it was a fine ambition, but I also added that I didn't think it possible for her to know what she wanted so early in life. As far as I was concerned it was all too sudden. Although I was very fond of Lois, I didn't think we should be so serious. Nevertheless, Winchell, Parsons, Hopper, Kilgallen, Wilson, Lyons, and all the other columnists from New York to California kept printing that we were engaged. Our pictures were in all the papers, generally on the first or third page.

A few days later, Lois's mother arrived from California and confirmed for me that Lois was sixteen after all. I was staggered. "She has always done exactly as she wanted," said the doting, indulgent, divorced mother. "But you are right, George, you certainly should wait a while before considering marriage."

We had known each other exactly three weeks. But what a three weeks. Lois, even at her tender age, was far more experi-

enced than women twice and three times her age. The newspapers
found our affair something to play with. What we did each night,
except in the bedroom, and some reporters even asked about that,
was given more space in the dailies than the war in Europe. A bar-
rage of photographers followed us everywhere we went. This was,
to say the least, good for my ego.

I realized after another week or so that I *was* in love again,
and full of ambition. This vibrant young girl, content to stand in
the wings during my vaudeville appearances and radio shows,
wanted nothing but my company, a home and a child. By God, I
felt, that was something to live for and to work for again.

A few days later, a group of Brooklyn businessmen came to me
with a plan. I was to act as their front man in a deal to buy the then
Brooklyn Dodgers baseball club and all its farms.

George McLaughlin, acting for the Brooklyn Trust Company,
would be happy to do business with me. I had been a baseball fan,
and still am, ever since I was a bat boy for John McGraw and the
New York Giants when I was very young. McLaughlin wanted to
unload the club; it was losing money. I set out to get the financial
backing, and the entire deal, I discovered, could be handled for
less than half a million in cash. I immediately began to lay plans to
bring showmanship to baseball.

The parking lot across the street from Ebbets Field could be
used for a bowling alley and a Dodger nightclub where fun-loving
Leo Durocher could lead the band. I envisaged another replica of
Little Old New York. That night I had some more ideas and was
making millions on a Stork Club tablecloth with Lois at my side. I
felt I would be able to keep her in style. I contacted some interests
in Philadelphia and was told to come in, sign the papers, and pick
up the check the following week.

Armed with papers and lawyers, I went to Philadelphia at the
appointed hour. Add up all the jokes that have ever been told
about Philadelphia being dead, multiply them by a hundred, and
you will get an idea of how dead my meeting with my supposed
backers was. While we were traveling to Philadelphia, the Germans had taken Paris.

"The world is finished, at least Europe," moaned one vice-
president, glumly.

"Georgie, you must be crazy," said another. "Who could possibly think of anything as insignificant as baseball when we will be in a war very soon just to protect our shores?"

It sounded like good sense to me so I called off all my negotiations with McLaughlin. Brooklyn proceeded to win the pennant that year. The following year, even with, or because of, the global war then raging, you couldn't have bought the Dodgers for five million in cash.

I got some more bad news when I returned to New York. My radio show would not be extended. I knew by innuendoes that my escapade in Florida and my possible marriage to a teenager influenced the sponsor's decision. While they never came out and said that was the reason, it was typical of Madison Avenue and of the little boys who ran, and still do, the advertising agencies of the country.

(Apropos of this, I was once walking down Park Avenue with an advertising agency executive of my acquaintance. I remarked that I thought a new show his agency had produced for a cigarette sponsor was excellent. "What did you think of it, Bill?" I asked. "I won't know until the ratings are in," he replied, dead pan. Typical, even today.)

Many of my friends kept pleading with me not to marry Lois after they heard of the cancellation. They said that, no matter how beautiful and adroit she was, I would be making a mistake. Just as many told me that, if it would make me happy, I should go ahead and take the plunge. "You are not going to hurt anyone but yourself if it doesn't work out," they counseled. I agreed.

Then came another hitch. Lois's father, although divorced from her mother, had neither been asked for his consent, nor would he give it. We could not be married in New York because there was some doubt as to the validity of Norma's Mexican divorce. I immediately arranged for an engagement in Detroit, as I heard that Michigan was less strict in its marriage laws regarding minors.

Lois and I, accompanied by mutual friends—I had to consider the Mann Act—flew to the Motor City, and photographers and reporters mobbed us at the airport. We were to be married that night, we told them. That is, until the judge who was to marry us decided he wanted some publicity and his pictures in the papers. He told the reporters we had to wait five days under an old law he had dug up somewhere.

We were married five days later. In retrospect, it wasn't a very romantic scene. Jimmy Cromwell, an old friend and our ambassador to Canada, flew down to act as my best man, and Gus Newman's Orchestra, from the nightclub in which I was appearing, supplied the music. No fewer than seventy photographers attended the ceremony and never stopped flashing their bulbs in our faces. It was a carnival.

Returning to New York, we made preparations to go to California. I had a three-day date in Philadelphia so I put Lois on the *Mercury*—God, my airline and travel bills in those days—to rent a house in Hollywood. Two days later Lois telephoned me that she had rented a house in the Hollywood Hills and asked when I would be out. I told her I was leaving that night.

Upon seeing the house Lois had rented, I immediately dubbed it the House That Karloff Built. The previous tenants had smashed practically all the furniture, and the house had a haunted feeling about it even though the house and grounds were beautiful. Even weeks after we were settled, the mice insisted on having breakfast with us. It was also necessary to hire security guards because sightseers were continually walking around the grounds peering in open windows trying to get a glimpse of us. They even tried to photograph us through the windows.

Then, three days after my arrival, the entire right side of my face became paralyzed and I was under the daily supervision of a doctor. A fine honeymoon for a girl of sixteen, married to a guy she knew was in love with the past, many years her senior, with very little money, and now with a paralyzed face; the future looked anything but rosy.

14

The Rocky Road of Matrimony

THREE months later I was back to normal and arranged a vaudeville tour with a company of such names from the motion picture
industry as Rochelle Hudson, Jean Parker, Isabel Jewel, and
others. Even in towns where I hadn't appeared before, there was
great interest in me and the show, thanks to the publicity of the
radio comedians such as Burns and Allen, Cantor, and Red Skelton. Cantor's most quoted crack was, "George Jessel was to be
here tonight but he couldn't make it. His wife is teething."

Red Skelton came on stage where an animal act had left a
small puddle and cracked, "Jessel's wife must have been here."
Milton Berle's quip was usually, "I get to the theater earlier than
Jessel because he has to take his wife to school first." George Burns
and Gracie Allen were widely quoted: "Tonight is maid's night out.
Jessel had to stay home and baby-sit his wife."

But Jack Benny, always the gentleman and a great man,
wasn't so cruel. He asked my permission to include a gag or two on
his show, but they weren't nearly so biting as the others. Only Fred
Allen left us untouched.

It got to the point where I had to have a picture of Lois placed in front of the theaters at which we appeared and call the audience's attention to it. "Any of those radio comics who have been kidding me about my wife should put a picture of theirs alongside mine and then we'll see who should laugh." When that remark started being quoted in the newspapers and columns, the snide cracks almost disappeared. Nevertheless, I have been the subject of many "young girl jokes" ever since.

But let me say here and now, and this may sound like Confucius—but it isn't, it is strictly Jessel: You can take it from me that all the cares of the world, no matter how great they are, are completely forgotten during the few seconds of an orgasm.

Lois finally decided to join me on the tour, and I paid her $600 a week just so the audience could see that she wasn't walking around in diapers and with a lollipop in her mouth.

In Miami we played a theater engagement for one week, but I suddenly felt during that time that Lois was no longer enamored of me. The first fascination, my being a different kind of guy than she had ever known, had worn off. That honeyed look in her eyes seemed to be missing. Intuitively, as with Norma several years before, I knew it had gone sour. It wasn't long after that that Lois told me so herself.

We had a fight, a beauty. I took a walk on the beach and bumped into Winchell. "Georgie, I'm so happy to hear your marriage is going so well. I'm saying so in my column tomorrow."

I rushed upstairs to Lois and made her laugh. "Honey, we can't split now. I wouldn't cross Winchell for anything!"

I gambled too much and had to telephone New York for work. Within an hour, Lois and I were booked into the Orpheum Theater in downtown Los Angeles. One morning she told me the news, which, under the circumstances of a few months before, would have been manna from heaven. She thought she was pregnant. She would go to the doctor that day and confirm it. There was little I could say because her attitude gave no indication whether she still wanted a baby or not. Between shows the next day, she came from the doctor's and burst into the dressing room with an expression only a very young girl can have. I was afraid she was going to say, "Thank God, I'm not pregnant."

Instead, she shouted, "It's true. I am going to have a baby," and she jumped around the room like a child on Christmas morning.

The next day I paid a deposit of $3,000 on a house in Brentwood we wanted to buy. Much to my sorrow, a few weeks later I had to sell it while still in escrow and recovered only a third of my $3,000. We decided it was too big; also, Lois could not sign any deeds or documents under the laws of that time. She was still a minor, married or not. (Thank God, the comedians didn't hear about *that*.)

There was a dinner to be given in honor of Louis B. Mayer and I was asked to be toastmaster. I did not accept at first but agreed to let the committee know later that day. I told Lois, "How can I talk sincerely and honestly knowing that, after it's over, no matter how much my speech is applauded, these film moguls will forget about me as soon as they reach their offices." I knew that if I stayed in California I would either have to pick oranges or starve.

"Try once more," said Lois, who really wanted to stay in California. "Just don't insult them no matter how great the temptation may be."

A few days later I found myself on the dais at the Hotel Biltmore flanked by all the Hollywood big shots. Seated at my right was Archbishop Cantwell of Los Angeles. As I introduced the speakers, I knew that each one was terribly jealous of Mayer and many of them genuinely loathed the man. I knew personally that most of them went out of their way to condemn him in their offices each hour of the day. Yet, here they were, jumping to their feet, hurling superlatives at Benevolent Uncle Louie, making him everything he wasn't, nor ever could be, a combination of General Pershing, Marshall Foch, and one of them even threw in a little Lincoln. I whispered to the archbishop sitting next to me:

"Your Grace, will you take me into confession for a moment?"

"What is it, my son?" he asked, eyes twinkling.

"I feel that this is an opportunity I have been waiting for for a long time. I would like to get up and address these picture executives and say, 'Now that I have you all together, may I tell you that you are the most insincere and phony bunch of bastards ever born to women!'"

"Peace, my son," said the startled archbishop, and I took his advice.

On October 22, 1941, Jerilynn was born, weighing in at six and a half pounds. The newspapers were full of it again, only this time with wholesome publicity. I was in New York preparing to produce a musical, *High Kickers*, with money I borrowed all over the country, including some from Tommy Manville and his Palm Beach friends, some more from Al Bloomingdale and Lee Shubert. Sophie Tucker was going to star with me.

My mother-in-law telephoned me from the coast with the news of Jerilynn. Lois wrote me endearing letters, and between the opening of *High Kickers* in Wilmington and the hiatus before we opened in New York, I flew to the coast to see my child for the first time.

Jerilynn was almost as pretty as her mother with one exception—a little quirk in the shape of her mouth that she inherited from me. Her beauty she inherited from Lois's genes, thank goodness.

The New York run of *High Kickers* was playing to good houses, but we lost money because it was an expensive show to maintain and sustained heavy losses on the road. I did the best I could to make Lois—and the baby—happy. I bought jewelry and clothes for Lois, not knowing when I would be able to pay for them.

After the show closed in New York, the road show flopped, too, and we closed in Chicago. I was broke again with nothing in the wind. But, as usual, something appeared on the horizon. I received a telephone call from Paul Small, a theatrical agent, later to be very big in Hollywood, telling me that he had an important proposition he wanted to discuss with me. The proposition was so good, said Paul, that on signing the contract, I would immediately get $10,000 in cash.

When Paul met me in Chicago, he told me how it all came about. It concerned another lothario who would rather play the balcony scene than make a bank deposit. His name was Fred Finkelhoffe, a man who had written the Broadway smash *Brother Rat* and several screenplays. Small and Fred had flown out to the coast together, and over a game of gin rummy, Fred told Paul he was depressed because he had recently met the Scotch lass Ella Logan while she was appearing in a Broadway hit. Though they were in

love, Ella, an independent woman, refused to come to the coast unless she had a job waiting.

Small, who could sell ice to Eskimos, had a solution. Vaudeville, because of wartime conditions, was coming back. He and
Finkelhoffe would produce a show for Los Angeles and put Ella in a
costarring position. No matter what happened to the show, Ella
would at least be close to him and they could be married.

"Paul," said Fred, "I'll do it provided you can get my favorite
performer to head the show."

"Who is he?" replied Paul, gingerly.

"Georgie Jessel."

"That'll be a cinch," laughed Paul. "Jessel is flat on his ass
again, and for a little money, he'll sign anything."

I told Paul I would agree to it, but I felt it was a crime because
Fred would be taken for a ride, especially for a show in a non-
theater town like Los Angeles. "Don't make with the philosophy,"
said Paul, as he chewed on one of my few remaining cigars. "Sign
the contract and here's the cash," pushing $10,000 across the table
at me.

The show opened at the Biltmore in Los Angeles with Jack
Haley, Ella, Kitty Carlisle, the De Marcos, Buck and Bubbles, Con
Colleano, and myself. Due to the advance Fred had given me, I was
many lengths in front of the sheriff for a change, and I would wake
up every morning happy with the thought that my daughter
Jerilynn could laugh at the world.

The opening night in Los Angeles was one of the greatest
demonstrations of audience approval I have ever known. This
reaction was more important than the average opening, for the audience consisted of a virtual Who's Who of radio and pictures. In
the front row were Jack and Mary Benny, Eddie Cantor, Al Jolson,
Mickey Rooney, Abbott and Costello, Charlie Chaplin, Burns and
Allen, and many, many others of their ilk. They and the rest of the
audience, when they weren't watching the show, stared at Lois
front row center.

The newspapers were extravagant in their praise. Damon
Runyon devoted an entire column to me and the entire cast of
Show Time. Every film company in Hollywood wanted to make a
test of Lois after seeing her on the stage at the final curtain call to

146 THE WORLD I LIVED IN

which I had summoned her. She made a test at Fox, and they immediately signed her to a contract. Lois made one picture under that contract, *Brenda Starr, Girl Reporter*.

But my happiness was to be short-lived. One night while driving home, she looked at me and quite calmly said, "Honey, you know I don't love you anymore. When are you going to move out?" I was stunned and speechless, although I must admit now that I wasn't very surprised. I had known it was coming; it was just a matter of time from that day in Miami Beach when I ran into Winchell.

A few days later I moved to the Biltmore; my pride more than my heart was hurt. I felt everyone was looking at me and saying, "There goes Jessel. Thrown out again!"

We dined after the show several times after that, but we both knew it was over. I did my best to win her back, but it was no good. Lois had taken up with a musician at Fox, and it was quite a love, according to her friends. We signed papers for the divorce to proceed and said goodbye very amicably.

I had to take the show to San Francisco, and Emmett Callahan, general manager for Finkelhoffe, informed me that we were going direct from San Francisco to New York with the show. This was, to me, the most insane showmanship I had ever heard. I thought to myself: "Here is a show that runs two and a half hours, and I am on the stage for more than half of that time, with the same jokes I had told in *High Kickers* and they laid an egg. So, they are going to take me back to Broadway and to the same theater, the Broadhurst."

"It's mad," I told Callahan. "Even though the rest of the show is fine, the critics will murder you on account of me. With the exception of George Jean Nathan, who has always liked me, they will kill us. You won't have a chance."

There was no talking to me about anything. Callahan and Finkelhoffe were adamant. I was really down in the dumps again. Both Small and Callahan, I was told later, telephoned Eddie Cantor in Los Angeles saying that I was terribly upset and begged him to fly to San Francisco and spend some time with me.

The next night I made the rounds of the saloons along the waterfront with a detective pal from the old days. Then we hit

Chinatown, not the places everyone went to, but the real Chinatown. In one of the restaurants, there sat in a dark corner a girl who looked half Chinese, or less. She was tall and dressed as if she had just stepped out of an I. Magnin window in a black sheath, and on her head a turban, the ends of which formed a scarf around her throat. I stared, fascinated, at this mysterious looking and lovely creature who returned my stares just as intently.

As I passed her table, I said "Good night." She returned it. The next night I noticed she was in the front row during the performance. After the show, she came backstage and we had supper together in my apartment at the Clift Hotel, one of the most comfortable hostelries in the western hemisphere, even today.

During supper, Sam Hearn, who gave me the train fare back to New York following my Marilyn Miller fiasco, who was then in San Francisco in another show, came up to the room complete with his violin. As he played, my oriental partner danced to the music of Rimski-Korsakov, and I remarked at her sensuous talent.

"Oh, you should see me dance when I'm not dressed this way." A thoughtful pause. "Do you want to stay up late?" she asked.

"Of course I do," I replied. It was only 4:00 A.M. She had also brought me a bottle of some exotic liqueur that most of the musicians in the show would have given up their union cards for. I was feeling no pain.

"Wait a few minutes," she murmured, "and I'll be right back."

Within half an hour, she had returned in a Chinese costume, tiny slippers, mandarin coat, the works, and had even brought along a mandarin coat for me. She danced while Sam played his fiddle for at least an hour. Sam eventually tired and took his leave, and I donned the pajamas, slippers, and mandarin coat that magically appeared from her bag. She put all the pillows she could find on the floor and sat close to me like a slave girl, cooing some Chinese lullaby. About nine, the telephone rang. It was Cantor.

"I'm downstairs, kiddo. I just flew in from L.A. because I heard you were sick and depressed. I've got my doctor with me and we're coming up. . . ." Before I had a chance to explain, he hung up.

If you ever saw Cantor's eyes pop on the screen, when he walked in that room they were twice their normal size. I was propped up high on the pillows like a Chinese nobleman, this very lovely creature at my feet singing. I had stage managed our positions for Eddie's benefit.

Eddie was speechless for a moment or two, then turned to the doctor. "This, I did not expect. So long, doc, I'll see you in L.A.— and you can send the bill to Jessel, under the circumstances."

I don't think the clean-living Eddie ever got over that scene, God rest his soul.

There were ten days between the closing of the show in San Francisco and the opening in New York. I flew to Los Angeles and took Jerilynn and her nurse to lunch at Romanoff's. It was that same day I started entertaining our soldiers, traveling in an army bus to March Air Force Base in Riverside County, where I did two shows that night. On the way back I stopped for the late papers. Lois had divorced me.

Although we had our respective representatives give out statements to the effect that we could not get along because I lived only for the theater, I had a feeling that the newspapers would give me a little the worst of it.

Under the circumstances, Lois and her mother had a difficult time in court, as they found it very hard to relate any "cruelty" on my part. Her mother told the judge that I had called Lois several names because of jealousy. Then, with tear-dimmed eyes, according to Louella Parsons, she hastily added, "But I know he didn't mean it!"

The attorneys and reporters threw in some interpolations that came out, "He's not too old for me, but I am too young for him." The newspapers around the country made the most of that phrase, and they still do.

The divorce agreement called for reasonable alimony and child support, and I was granted custody of Jerilynn for four months during the summer after she reached five years of age. After I said goodbye to Lois, her mother, and Jerilynn, tearfully, I stopped at the Polo Lounge of the Beverly Hills Hotel for a drink, or two or three.

After my fourth gin and Dubonnet, I found myself listening to the soft murmur of an English voice with blonde hair falling over her face a la Veronica Lake. Then, I spotted a young leading man I knew and asked him if he knew the young lady. He did and I was introduced to Lady Billie Rapheal, who turned out to be very sympathetic to my tales of woe about being separated from my only child and Lois. I was intrigued, also, by her conversation. She, too, was talking about a divorce from Lord Rapheal.

"Would it be too much if I requested your company to the airport? I have to leave for New York in an hour," I told her, wishing it were twenty-four hours because I could see something building up with this young and lovely English lass.

"Come, I'll drive you," she replied, and she did in the smartest, biggest Rolls-Royce I had ever seen. On the way to Burbank, she told me she had pleaded with her husband not to come to Hollywood on business. She was certain it would break up their marriage.

It had.

We had another drink in the Sky Room and delayed my departure until the very last minute. I left on the evening *Mercury.*

Billie followed three hours later on TWA.

I should add an amusing anecdote about something that happened before we left for the airport. Billie and I had more or less planned for her to take TWA to New York because the *Mercury* sleeper flight, on which I was booked, was full. Before leaving the Beverly Hills Hotel, I accompanied Billie to her room to pack her bags.

She had been dating one of her husband's jockeys after the split with him, and just as we were coming out of her room, the jockey, Sammy Rennick, was coming up the corridor. Billie told Sammy we were leaving for New York and that she would telephone him when she arrived. We left Sammy standing there astonished, staring at our backs.

All of a sudden he ran after us, planted his feet, and kicked Billie square in the bottom, turned around and laughed uproariously. After the momentary shock had left us, so did we.

15

Hollywood–Again

In New York I was informed that Lucille Norman would replace Kitty Carlisle and that Tony and Sally de Marco decided to stick with the show instead of remaining in Los Angeles. Buck and Bubbles, who couldn't make it because of prior commitments, were replaced by another act. Ella Logan left Fred again. He was felled by his own axe, so to speak.

My attorney, following my divorce from Lois, investigated my accounts and found that I still owed $56,000 to various and sundry people, including the government. He felt a good run in *Show Time* would take care of them. But I was still skeptical about its—and my—success.

Billie arrived and checked in at the Sherry Netherland in an adjoining room, and we immediately took off for a weekend at Billy Rose's magnificent country estate. Weekends with the Roses (Eleanor Holm) usually included such scintillating company as the Leonard Lyons, the Nicky Blairs, Ben and Rose Hecht, Tex and Jinx (Falkenberg) McCrary, and others of their ilk. This particular weekend, Orson Welles showed up, and we have been firm friends ever since.

Lady Billie and I had a strange time. We knew when we met at the Polo Lounge that we had not fallen in love with each other. It seemed our mutual attitudes and physical attraction for each other had made itself evident to the Rose ménage, particularly Orson. Immediately after being introduced, he proceeded to go on the make for her and continued his pursuit until she returned to London and eventually married again. Nevertheless, it was a lovely interlude with a lovely English girl. But on to business—for a change. I had to make some bank deposits, not continually play the balcony scene.

As I mentioned, I told Callahan and Finkelhoff I felt the show would bomb in New York because of the *el foldo* done by *High Kickers* with my using some of the same material. My pals and my beloved mother were worried about my being nervous and upset for the opening. Generally, on such occasions, I was very calm. I even had my doctors, pals since childhood, in the dressing room with me while I made up for my first entrance. They helped a great deal by playing high stakes gin rummy with me kibitzing; so much so I almost missed my first cue.

In the front row for the first night I spotted Mr. and Mrs. Vincent Astor, the Jules Brulators, Orson (with Billie, if you please), Elsa Maxwell, Maxie Rosenbloom, and many others of New York first-night society. Murderers Row on the aisles was fully occupied with the first string from every New York paper. I need not have worried about them.

I kidded about *High Kickers* and had the audience in stitches. I thought I even spied a smile from some of the critics. I know I did from George Jean Nathan. I felt then that we were "in." My fears—and predictions—were all wrong. They loved us. The audience and critics received us as well as they did in Los Angeles and San Francisco. As far as I was concerned, personally, they had never been nicer to me. The same jokes and bits that had laid an egg in *High Kickers* were tremendous standouts in *Show Time*. The same critics who had condemned or damned me with faint praise for that show, hurled such superlatives as, "This is the master entertainer of them all." Brooks Atkinson wrote, "I left 'Show Time' before the curtain fell. It is now several hours later and, possibly, Mr. Jessel is still on the stage. If he is, I know the audience is still rocking with laughter."

Louis Sobol wrote, "The funniest man on the stage is George Jessel in 'Show Time'." George Jean Nathan, who always liked me, said, "Georgie Jessel is the world's greatest monologist." I noticed that he doubled over at the Professor Larbermarcher routine. It had always made him laugh.

So, at long last, I had a hit on Broadway. After all the years I struggled, this moment was worth it. If ever a man had been close to the breaking point, it had been me after *High Kickers* folded in Chicago.

I stayed with the show for six months, my debts were paid, and I was happy again. I was to be made even happier during the run of the show when old pal Joe Schenck came to visit me backstage toward the end of my run. "George, I think Fox could use you and your talents on the coast in pictures again. You have never reached your peak in the business.

"Darryl [Zanuck] is in Washington and being mustered out of the army. He'll be in New York next week and wants to see you."

(If you will recall, I had first run across the man I consider a true motion picture genius—giant, if you will—so many years before when he was at Warner Brothers as production assistant to Jack Warner. He had, of course, formed 20th Century-Fox and had discovered Shirley Temple, who saved the studio from bankruptcy in the mid and late thirties. I felt I would like to make a few pictures for this man.)

But Joe, a few minutes later, was to leave me speechless. I had misinterpreted his remarks. "I think you would make a damn fine producer and creator of musical films for us and I'll let Darryl talk to you about it."

I thought about Joe's remarks many times before I met Darryl again. I had always been unlucky in Hollywood, having been hired and fired by practically every studio—sometimes my fault, sometimes theirs. I told Joe that I would think it over until I saw him again in a few days and that I would have dinner with Darryl at the Stork when he arrived.

It turned out Darryl had read *S' Help Me*, a book I had written about my early years in show business and he liked it. I still had visions of performing in a few pictures. Darryl was to tell me otherwise.

"How would you like to get rid of all those funny clothes and wigs, sit behind a desk, and try to produce motion pictures? I'll give you a good chance, a seven-year contract, with options, and you'll work very close to me. I think you will be good at it. . . ."

Before I could say anything, Zanuck added, "See Joe Moscowitz here in New York and work out a deal. No percentage, just a good salary."

I was as completely surprised as if someone had said, "I love the way you sing 'My Mother's Eyes.' You should be president of a bank."

I called all my cronies, and especially Sam Carlton. He advised me against the move, as did Lew Cooper, my booking agent. He said he could book me for a nationwide tour following the success of *Show Time* for three or four thousand a week.

But the rest of the boys heartily agreed with me, and so did Paul Small, who really started the whole chain working in the first place by knowing Finkelhoffe. He said, among other things, it would be nice for me to be near Jerilynn.

So, on June 12, 1943, accompanied by Sam, I rented a house in California near the studio, and on July 1, I was given an office and a secretary and some scripts to read. I didn't see Zanuck immediately, even though he had returned to the studio. I learned in a very short time that there were two Zanucks. One outside the office, gay and carefree, and the other in the office who fully concentrated on the business of making pictures from noon until midnight or three in the morning. I had made up my mind that I would go to Hollywood this time with the same feeling of authority that I had on the Broadway stage. But it didn't work out that way. I began to think I had made a mistake (again) in giving up Broadway for Never-Never Land. I started making speeches at many dinners in Hollywood and flying all over the country to preside at testimonials to keep my deflated ego alive. I held forth in the executive dining room by making with the jokes until people began murmuring behind my back, "Jessel is out here as Zanuck's court jester."

Then, one morning I read an item in, I believe, Lenny Lyons's column that 20th Century-Fox was considering a film based on the lives of the Dolly Sisters, whom I had known well and worked with many times in vaudeville over the years. Rose and Jenny Dolly had come to America from Hungary when they were kids and had become internationally famous as singers, dancers, and actresses, favorites of kings, dukes, earls, and millionaires. They had, on one occasion, broken the bank at Monte Carlo.

I made up my mind that if I could produce anything, it would certainly be a story based on the theater such as this. I rushed over to Darryl's office, ad-libbed a plot, and got the assignment, much to the chagrin of many other veteran line producers who had been working for Zanuck for years. I immediately called in my old friend from the *Izzy Murphy* days, Lloyd Bacon, as I knew he had a "feel" for the theater and the talent of "show folk." I set him as the director immediately—before another producer could grab him. I hired Marian Spitzer and John Larkin to write the screenplay from my ad-libbed plot.

I learned in a very short time that facts have nothing to do with entertainment, and that truth, though often stranger than fiction, is completely unimportant unless it can bring laughter or tears or both.

Also, the many gay things about the Dolly Sisters, such as their numerous love affairs, would not suit the requirements of the strict, silly, strangling censorship of the Hays Office of those days.

Nevertheless, we came up with an excellent script, and I started looking around for "The Dolly Sisters." I was told I would have to use contract stars and supporting players, and I immediately settled on Betty Grable and Alice Faye. I also heard about a young girl who was under contract who hadn't as yet been used in any big role. Her name was June Haver.

Zanuck and his "yes men," of which there were plenty, wanted Grable and Faye. But Alice, just at the crucial moment, decided to retire while she was still on top. I knew Grable and Faye would make excellent Dolly Sisters in spite of the fact that they were both blonde and their characters were brunettes in real life. Zanuck suggested I use another of the Fox contract players who had had experience. Because it is still a sore point with her, over thirty years later, I will not mention her name.

I wanted June Haver. Lloyd and I had made a secret test of her. It took the diplomacy of a latter-day Henry Kissinger to persuade Darryl to let me use this unknown, untried performer. When Darryl saw the test, he agreed I was right. He gave me a look that told me I knew what I was doing. We never argued over my casting after that. The film turned out to be great entertainment and did tremendous business all over the world. The late Billy Wilkerson, founder-publisher of the *Hollywood Reporter*, threw every orchid he could my way. I was off to a flying start.

I also starred June in *I Wonder Who's Kissing Her Now,* and this film put her in the top rank of Fox stars. June is, today, happily married to Fred MacMurray.

Following another musical, *Do You Love Me,* I then tackled, at Darryl's request, *Nightmare Alley,* from William Gresham's blood-curdling story about carnival "geeks." No other line producer would touch it. The story and film were years ahead of their time, and it should have starred a fellow like Brando rather than Tyrone Power.

The part was played beautifully by Ty, and I'll never forget the reaction of an audience in Dallas when the picture was sneaked there. Power, the villain, did everything wrong for a human being. The Dallas (and every other) audience had never seen Ty in anything in which he didn't play the hero or the lover. When a young acrobat in the film attacked Power for trying to seduce a sweet, innocent young girl, while also carrying on an affair with a married woman, the kids in the audience yelled, "Knock him down, Ty!" I knew then the film didn't stand a chance.

It was in *When My Baby Smiles at Me,* a new title for the play *Burlesque,* that I introduced a new team—Betty Grable and Dan Dailey. In my humble opinion, these two stars gave the best performances of their lives, and the public agreed with me. They went on to star in many more films together. In *Wait 'till the Sun Shines, Nellie,* David Wayne gave the most brilliant performance of any actor I had ever seen until then. But David's great talent would not be recognized until he scored on Broadway in *Teahouse of the August Moon.* But my favorite discovery during my eleven years at Fox was Mitzi Gaynor.

Mitzi made three excellent films for me, *I Don't Care* with David Wayne, followed by *Golden Girl* with Dale Robertson, and then *Bloodhounds over Broadway.* Mitzi was the sole star in all three films. She has gone on to great heights in the business, and I am very proud to have discovered her talent first.

I was riding high again and I had never been happier. I was

dating Carole Landis, with whom I had a long-lasting affair until she met Rex Harrison and died so tragically. It was so unnecessary; I felt she had a future, albeit a modest one, in films and she was fairly well off financially as far as I knew.

While Carole never did make a picture for me, I did want her to star in *Dancing in the Dark*. I was stymied because of studio politics. Zanuck wanted to sign Cary Grant for two pictures, but Cary would not agree unless we guaranteed to star his then wife Betsy Drake in a film or two. I was stuck with her. Instead of starring Carole in the film, who had the experience, the name, the voice, and the camera know-how for a tight schedule, I was forced to use Betsy.

The role called for a well-built young lady to star with Bill Powell in a backstage show business story. After seeing Betsy in the first few days' rushes, I was aghast. She had no bosom or cleavage whatsoever. When I mentioned this to the wardrobe department, they said she refused to wear any, shall I say, padding in the vital spots. I went upstairs to see Darryl about this. He always liked full-bodied women.

"Darryl," I moaned, "this is the first time in the history of motion pictures that I have an electrician on the set with bigger tits than the leading lady!"

Even though he laughed uproariously over my remarks, he insisted I stick with Betsy and use her in the film. "I need Grant for two pictures, George; that's all there is to it. You know how these things are."

I took out my frustration by firing the electrician and hiring one with no tits so he wouldn't show her up. Nevertheless, *Dancing in the Dark* made a lot of money for Fox.

All in all, I produced twenty-four pictures for 20th Century-Fox, the hits far outnumbering the failures. I have to say in retrospect that my ten-odd years with Darryl and 20th Century-Fox were easily the most fruitful of my long career in show business. I proved to Hollywood, to Broadway, to the Warners, to the Mervyn Le Roys, the Rogers, the Lessers, Cowdins, and Sheehans, and all the rest of them, that I did know what I was doing. But it was Joe Schenck, God rest his soul, and Darryl Zanuck, truly a motion picture genius, who found out what I could do best—and let me do it my way.

The security of a long-term contract gave me a clarity of mind and allowed me to use many resources that had never been tapped before. I was able to be active in many charitable and benevolent organizations; I spoke on two occasions to a group of men and raised the money to build two houses of worship; I created—with Bing Crosby who never set foot in the place—the Friars Club of California. It hurt me when, many years later, some criminal card cheats used the club to bilk many, many fine people out of millions of dollars at gin rummy. I believe one or two of them are still in jail.

The Friars arranged one performance at the Shrine Auditorium in Los Angeles from which we were able to present a check to the Motion Picture Relief Fund for over $300,000. Being a film producer made me the recipient of more New Year's greetings in one year than I had received in a lifetime on Broadway. It also brought many beautiful girls to my attention, to my arms, and to my bed.

I escorted Marilyn Monroe to her first big Hollywood party at the Beverly Wilshire Hotel, a party in honor of Henry Ford. I arranged for Marilyn to be decked out in a beautiful maroon velvet dress from the wardrobe department, with a makeup man and hairdresser to take care of the rest. When we walked into the ballroom, every face in the place was turned in our direction, including Ford's. There wasn't a man present who didn't receive a dirty look, or an elbow in the ribs, from his wife or girlfriend because of the attention he was paying to Marilyn; several bus boys dropped their trays.

I also became engaged to another tragic figure, Abigail "Tommy" Adams. Tommy, as she was known to everyone, was a playgirl who never made it to the top in Hollywood. An early divorce from actor Lyle Talbot convinced her she was a failure as a wife. On the sound stages of Hollywood, she met with even less success. At the age of twenty-seven, she was still considered a "starlet" by Harry Cohn at Columbia. Even the patient Harry dropped Tommy's final option as an actress and, apparently, the option on her life as well.

Tommy didn't need the salary from Columbia. She had a large personal income. Stardom and recognition were what she sought. Lack of talent as an actress was her one and only, but biggest,

drawback. (All the money in the world can't provide you with acting talent, or talent in any of the arts. It is either born into you, or
it is not. Drama schools and coaches, with extremely rare excep-
tions, cannot teach you to act; they can only develop latent talent
and teach you how to move.)

Tommy and I went around for several years and planned to
be married. After Harry dropped her option, she continually
threatened suicide, and many times, while I was on the road for
Fox plugging films, or making speeches, I had to call George
Fisher, the CBS Radio Network motion picture editor, and a close
friend, to rush to Tommy's apartment after she had telephoned me
and said she was going to end it all. I think George must have
smashed down three or four doors to the apartment I rented for
Tommy in Hollywood.

We were engaged for several months; that is, until Tommy
started on the deadliest parlay known to medical science—booze
and barbiturates. She became a common barfly after we broke up.
Three times in 1954 she was arrested for drunk driving. Each time
she came away from court saying, "Never again. I'm going to
marry George and settle down." We never got around to marrying.
Perhaps if we had, things would have been different for Tommy.
She finally made good on her suicide threats. The final time she
never called me.

Perhaps one thing that stands out in my Zanuck decade, and
perhaps the most important, is when I acted as public relations
liaison for Darryl on a splendid motion picture, *Wilson*, based on
the life of the World War I president. The picture didn't make any
money, but it did an awful lot of good, and the picture business was
in such good shape that it didn't hurt to make such a picture. A few
westerns and a musical or two would repay the costs in a few
months.

Darryl and I went to the White House to show the film to FDR
personally. I was happy to be able to renew my friendship with the
president, as we hadn't met since the Litvinoff dinner. When the
film was over, he lionized Zanuck. Although FDR could smile and
not always mean it, he certainly did after seeing *Wilson*. I can still
see him, even now, in his chair, with his arm around Darryl.
"Colonel, what has Georgie Jessel got to do with this film?"

With an apology, I interrupted and said: "Mr. President, I have been very anxious about this picture and feel it is good for the world to see such a film. Not only that, I have ambitions for Mr. Zanuck. If he sets his mind to it, some day he, too, may be president and then I'll be the Jim Farley of his administration!"

FDR broke up and almost choked on his cigarette holder.

Among the special group that had been invited to see the film was a retiring little man in a seersucker suit from Kansas City whom I had met many years before when he was with the Pendergast machine in Kansas City. We got to talking again, remembering the old days.

"I thought the picture was wonderful. I wanted to tell Colonel Zanuck so, but I think he feels I don't like him."

I asked Senator Harry Truman why he felt this way.

"Well," he replied, "he thinks I slighted him in some army report."

I explained to Harry that Darryl never mentioned it to me and that they ought to straighten it out right now. I went over to Darryl and introduced them. "Darryl, you know Senator Truman, don't you?" They shook hands and were friendly to the end. Bygones were bygones.

After the Truman–White House episode, Darryl and I became more than extremely friendly; we became very intimate friends. I knew, of course, that Darryl was engaging in many extra-curricular activities here and in Europe. His wife, Virginia, took it all in her stride and knew that one day Darryl would come home. (He did, in a tearful reconciliation in Palm Springs twenty years later. Today, in the twilight of their lives, they are very happy together.)

Anyway, knowing my penchant for words—I had often told Darryl of my "Indian Love Lyrics" ploy—Darryl had me writing love letters from him to his various *amours* around the world.

After writing several of these—very successfully for Darryl —and at least one a week, he asked me to write one to Joan Fontaine who had starred in several pictures for Darryl, including *Island in the Sun*, which was made in the Caribbean. Darryl had been chasing Joan around the palm trees in the Bahamas for weeks. Luckily for her, Joan was sharing a room with fellow costar Patricia Owens and never alone.

I composed one of my better missives to Joan and expressed undying admiration for Darryl of her charms. I had my secretary mail the letter that evening. Two weeks later I received a very irate telephone call, to say the least, from Joan, who didn't know what it was all about.

"What the hell are you writing me love letters for? We've never even dated. How dare you?" (I must admit it was a rather passionate letter.) It turned out I had inadvertently signed my own name to it. I have never been able to write very well because of my lack of education; I always had the letters typewritten, and my secretary must have slipped this one in accidentally and I signed it.

Thinking fast, and realizing this is what I had done, I told Joan someone else had been sending such letters to various young ladies around town and this must be one of them. Joan, lady that she is, accepted this explanation. But Darryl often wondered why she never answered "his letter." I never told him why.

Of all the people I've known and worked for in show business, I say, without hesitation, that Darryl was the finest. He was a very good friend, a genius at producing motion pictures. I am only too happy for Darryl and Virginia that they are back together, and obviously for the rest of their lives, living very happily on the Zanuck estate in Palm Springs. As soon as I heard that Darryl had "come home" from Europe, I rushed to Palm Springs and saw him for the first time in many years. It was a very tearful, emotional reunion. I hope I have many more with this fine man from Wahoo, Nebraska.

One more self-effacing note on my tenure at Fox that concerns Virginia and her interest in the company her husband founded. She called me one day at the studio and asked me if I would read a book called *Leave Her to Heaven.* She felt it would make a fine motion picture.

I read it and immediately bought it for Fox. Every producer on the lot, including Darryl, was against it. Their reaction was that an audience would not go for it because the leading lady was a villainess. "They'll hate her," was the general reaction around the executive lunch table.

Nevertheless, future events proved me—and Virginia—right. The picture was a smash, and Gene Tierney became an international star as a result of *Leave Her to Heaven.*

16

Harry Truman—Again

FOLLOWING my meeting with FDR and Harry Truman with Darryl, I met up with Harry Truman once again, immediately after he was inaugurated as vice-president at the start of FDR's fourth term. I had been asked to be toastmaster at the banquet for that occasion and had been bested in a battle of wits by Eleanor Roosevelt earlier in the day.

During my speech in welcoming the audience of senators, congressmen, and their wives, I said something to the effect: "We are beginning the speeches much earlier than we had planned, and I knew this would happen, because I knew all of you would rush to the tables, have lunch, and become very hungry. I, too, lunched at the White House today, and never in my life have I seen so much lettuce surrounding so little chicken. And while I know that the first lady of the land is so apt in so many things, if the chicken salad is any sign at all, she is not a very good cook."

A little later on, when I presented Mrs. Roosevelt, she topped me with: "I am sure Georgie is mistaken. I don't remember putting *any* chicken in the chicken salad!"

After dinner that evening, some of us had an extra cup of coffee in the anteroom with General Marshall, General Omar Bradley, Mr. and Mrs. Truman, Fred Vinson, and some other Democratic party bigwigs. Harry and I sat and conversed in a corner and talked about the days when I had first met him. I also told him about my reviving the song "I'm Always Chasing Rainbows" in one of my upcoming films. Harry immediately jumped up and went to the piano and played a little Chopin, the melody from which the song was taken.

It was some time before I was to see him again. I was in my office at 20th Century-Fox and received a telephone call from another good friend, Bryan Foy, film producer *par excellence* of low budget pot-boilers, and the elder son of the illustrious Eddie Foy.

"George, a friend of ours took the rap for some other guys and has paid his debt to society. He is on parole and what he deserves is a clean bill of health, a pardon."

"What the hell can I do about it, Brynie," I asked him, mystified.

"Well, we've got to do something before the election. Much as I don't want it to happen, it looks like Dewey will win in a landslide over Harry Truman. I don't know any of *them* well enough to ask whether or not they can help.

"Why don't you join the Democratic Committee with me, make a few speeches, and some of the big shots might help us in getting a pardon. [He] did get a raw deal. . . ."

A few days later, in the *Los Angeles Herald-Express*, there was a small item about Harry Truman coming to California to make some political speeches, adding that I would introduce him at Gilmore Field, the old Hollywood Stars baseball park—now the site of CBS Television City.

An hour or so later I received another telephone call from one of the executives of Fox, the political contact. "George, your politics belong to you, but in your speech at Gilmore Field and in any other speeches you make for Truman, don't give the impression you are speaking for Fox or the industry in general. Most of us are Republicans, especially here. Anyway, do you *really* think this guy Truman has a chance?"

"I don't. . . ."

Before I had a chance to finish, he broke in with, "Why get yourself mixed up in something when you can't win!"

I thought it over and made up my mind that he was perfectly right. I wrote a letter to the *Herald* and said I had *not* been asked to introduce Truman by anyone who had such authority but that I would deem it a privilege to meet him again. I added I would also consider it a privilege to meet Governor Dewey of New York, Truman's opponent.

About two months later, Harry came to California. I received another telephone call from Brynie saying that he had met with the president in San Francisco and that he had asked for me.

This, I didn't believe! Then I received a call from Helen Gahagan Douglas, then engaged in a battle with Richard Nixon for the Senate, and she repeated the same thing. This, too, I didn't believe and figured that Brynie had told her to call me.

I told Helen I would think it over. On arriving at the office the next morning, there was an urgent telephone call from Truman's secretary Matt Connelly, in the course of which he said the president wanted to see me.

I went down to the Biltmore Hotel expecting to stand in line and shake hands along with a group of a few loyal Democrats, hardly any from the business with the exception of Ronald Reagan, the Bogarts, and one or two others.

Instead, I was taken to Harry's suite. When we were alone he said, "I want you to be with me tonight and say a few words if you will, George."

At the time Harry was going through hell. He was trying to be re-elected, or rather elected in his own right, almost single-handedly and was getting very little help from very few Democrats. His voice was almost gone, and I was later told that with almost every sentence he uttered, he would look toward Bess and his daughter Margaret as if to ask, "Are they hearing me?"

In reply to Truman's request, I tried to be as diplomatic as I could. "Mr. President, I know little of politics in California and am particularly ignorant of the state issues. I don't really think I can be of much help to you. This is too tense a campaign in which to inject humor or comic relief. This is about all I would have to offer."

Harry looked at me as if to say, "Another one deserting the ship." "Well, come on up with me, anyway," he pleaded.

About fifty of us had dinner, and then we were all asked to get in the twenty cars outside for a motorcade to Gilmore Field down Wilshire Boulevard and then Fairfax Avenue, the heart of the Los Angeles Jewish section. I was to ride with the president.

All along the route there were cries of "Give 'em hell, Harry!" "You can do it, Harry!" Never, I felt, had there been a president as popular with the little people as Harry S. Truman. But my hands were tied.

I tried to console him during the ride about the election —hypocritically, I suppose, because I did not see how he could win against the Dewey-Republican machine, hungry for the White House after sixteen years. I also added that he had done a great deal for the black population of the country and that no one else, including Roosevelt, and all the other presidents put together, had given anything but lip service to the blacks since Abraham Lincoln. This gave me an idea as to how I could get off the hook and still stay on his good side.

At the rally, I said simply, "I am happy to be in so close proximity to the man who holds the highest office in the land." In a few words I told the audience, more than half of which was black, what I had told Harry in the car. I summed it up by saying, "No other man in his position has so stuck his chin out to help any minority as Harry S. Truman!"

This, even though it doesn't sound like much, got a lot of applause. Following the rally, we had a drink and another chat. I put my arms around him before he left and said I knew the Lord would continue to bless him and said goodbye with a kiss on the cheek.

The rest is history. California was responsible for Harry's election in 1948. I never mentioned our friend to Harry, but I'm sure Brynie did, and my name was probably used in getting a pardon for him.

During the rest of his term and when he came to New York, I would often meet Harry (who credited me with a lot of his voter strength in Southern California) at 7:00 A.M., and we would walk along Fifth Avenue, and crowds would gather to heckle him or praise him. I also rode in his car to open the United Nations Building. I will never forget Harry S. Truman, and I will never forget his friendship.

During one meeting I had with him, a private lunch for the two of us at Blair House (the White House, during most of Harry's second, elected term, was undergoing rebuilding), he was on the telephone to Eisenhower in Paris while Ike was NATO commander. "That was Ike, George. He just told me that if he does run for president, it will be as a Democrat in 1952."

The closest I ever came to the White House during Ike's presidency was Baltimore. Very few people got in to see the Chairman of the Board, as he was referred to by most of his cronies. I have been the guest of every president in the White House since Coolidge with the exception of Eisenhower and Gerald R. Ford.

But of all the things that have happened to me, the warmest and most important pat on the back I ever received came from Harry S. Truman. At a public dinner in Washington, Harry rose and said, "As President of the United States, I would like to present to you the Toastmaster-General of our country, George Jessel."

I loved Harry S. Truman, a man of the people. There will never be another like him.

17

A Command Performance

AFTER almost eleven years at Fox, I could see my time was coming to an end. Television was beginning to ravage the industry as we had known it, Darryl was living in Europe, and many of the old executives were leaving and new, younger management was taking over.

Several times while I was at Fox Harry Cohn had discussed with me the possibility of my coming to Columbia when I left Fox. It was, I thought, a firm offer. Consequently, I resigned my contract six months before it was due to expire. Mainly this was because I wasn't feeling well and my doctor told me I needed an operation that would lay me up for several months.

After recuperating, I called Harry and told him I was ready to go to work again and would like to work out a contract. "Georgie, I can't afford you. Your kind of pictures would break Columbia."

Naturally, I was disappointed at Harry's decision, but as I have said many times over the years, Harry was a great showman but a son of a bitch. He died about a year after our conversation.

I then went on a cross-country tour to sell Bonds for Israel, which, thanks again to Harry Truman, became an independent state. I made many after-dinner speeches and tried television again

166

in a show called "The Hollywood Revue." Jimmy Durante and I alternated as hosts for NBC. The ratings were not good, and it was my appearance before a congressional committee in which I berated the ratings that had me banned almost entirely from network television. It is incomprehensible to me how approximately 1,200 people in this great country of ours of over 200,000,000—at least one-third of which own television sets—can decide what and who the television viewers of this country are going to be allowed to see on television.

It is similar to a pollster going down to the garment district in New York and asking three men what they had for lunch. If two of the three say they ate chopped liver and onions, then the polling company will announce, in screaming headlines and on the six o'clock news, that two of every three men in New York eat chopped liver and onions for lunch.

I proved my point about polls for television shows by telephoning, at their expense, several people at random around the country and asked them what their favorite television show was. One woman in Detroit said she always watched Jackie Gleason on Thursday night on NBC. (Gleason, of course, was always on on Saturday night and on CBS.) The woman was certain of this because Thursday night her husband played cards at his club and she could watch anything she wanted. This happened during several of the calls and impressed the committee, but to no avail for reform.

As I have said many times throughout this book and in public appearances, Madison Avenue dictates to this country and to Washington when it comes to who and what is seen on the air.

I will have more to say about the networks later on, particularly the affair with Edwin Newman on the "Today" show in 1971.

In October, 1955, the highlight of my career occurred, and a great honor was bestowed upon me. You will recall that very early in my career, I played the Victoria Palace in London with Lou Edwards during World War I and saw Buckingham Palace from the top of a bus.

Because of my many trips to England entertaining the troops during World War II, and my motion picture production activities, I always have been very well known in London.

I received a letter from the Variety Artists Benevolent Fund requesting, or rather commanding, my appearance at the Royal

Command Performance at the Victoria Palace Theater, the very same theater in which I had appeared with Lou so many years before. This is an annual event held to raise funds to care for indigent British variety performers. In the letter it stated I would be allowed six minutes for a monologue. The performance was to be held on November 7, 1955.

On the bill were such stalwarts of the British theater as Sir Laurence Olivier and the late Noel Coward. As a rule, they make everybody rehearse, instruct them how to bow, and implore them to make no references whatever to the Royal Family of any kind.

Because I was not sure what I was going to say that evening until I reached the theater, I told the producer, Jack Hilton, that it was not necessary for me to appear at the dress rehearsal, ". . . and you already know how I look in white tie and tails."

Jack, one of London's foremost impresarios and a former dance band leader, agreed. I had an arrangement made of "Yankee Doodle Dandy" the morning of the performance to be played as if it were taken from a symphony. It was a beautiful, stirring arrangement.

Halfway through my monologue, I turned to the royal box and said, "Your Majesties, two weeks ago I had no idea I would be commanded to your presence here tonight. I haven't been on a stage in many years." The audience, and Hilton in the wings, started to gasp.

Nevertheless, I continued over the buzz of the audience.

"I have confined my speaking activities to after-dinner speeches and the rest of my time to producing motion pictures. But because I write my own speeches I have become conversant with a great deal of English literature, particularly that of English poets from the days of Chaucer to Dylan Thomas. I am particularly intrigued with the melancholy poems of A. E. Houseman, and a few lines from one of his verses, which I dedicate to you, Your Majesty." The house started to quiet down.

> The stars are bright;
> The moon is light;
> The dales are bright between,
> and all because for many years,
> God will save the Queen!

This was recited, on cue, under that arrangement of "Yankee

Doodle Dandy,'' and by that time I had done nearly one-half hour, twenty-odd minutes more than I had been allotted by Hilton. It brought the house down and a wave of the hand from the Queen, a royal salute in their protocol.

Following the performance, all the stars were invited to the party that traditionally follows the performance. During the evening I found myself dancing a waltz with the Queen Mother, the mother of the present Queen, a charming, gracious and very beautiful woman in spite of her photographs, which never, to my mind, did her justice.

In the middle of the dance floor, with everyone looking on, the former Queen said to me:

"We were told you were going to make us laugh, Mr. Jessel, but I never knew you would touch us so emotionally.''

I was a little taken aback.

"Thank you, Your Majesty. Now may I tell you something? I doubt that I will ever be in such close proximity to you again.''

"Certainly, Mr. Jessel, please do.''

"If you had no title, Your Majesty, and I saw you on the street, I would turn around, chase you down an alley and whistle at you.''

Without batting an eyelid or arching a royal eyebrow, and in typical British understatement, the Queen Mother replied, very slowly,

"How cha . . . aa . . . r . . . ming.''

Apparently, my very bold statement to the former Queen of England, and her reply, was reported to the British papers by a press secretary, and only one took a knock at me. All the others came out and said, in effect, "The Queen Mother was spoken to like a woman!''

To my mind, she is a great and gracious lady and it was a highlight of my career. I had come a long way since that day when, from the top of a London bus, a budding Jewish comedian had seen Buckingham Palace and opened at the Victoria Palace of Varieties just a stone's throw away.

The following day I received a telephone call from A. P. Herbert, then still the venerated editor of *Punch*, who asked me if I could come to the Savoy Ballroom at one o'clock that day—it was already 10:30 A.M.—and speak at the seventieth or eightieth birthday testimonial to Somerset Maugham. (I forget which one it was.) A. P. told me that every bigwig in London would be there, including Sir Winston Churchill.

In London, at the time, Danny Kaye was a very big hit at the Palladium and was playing to SRO houses at every performance. His picture was in the paper nearly every day for something he had done, or was doing, for orphans, the United Nations, or some other very worthy cause. In addition, his escapist films during the war such as *Walter Mitty* were tremendously popular throughout Great Britain. In short, Danny Kaye was almost as big as Sir Winston to Londoners. (I had to bring this up so that you could understand the following.)

When Herbert asked me this, I was at a loss. "A. P., I normally prepare my speeches for anything at all two or three days before a function. You have given me about two hours to memorize a speech befitting such an individual as Maugham."

Herbert didn't hesitate. "Oh, George, we're sure you can find a few words to say, and Sir Winston has particularly asked that you be there after the performance last night."

I finally agreed, because I figured I could have some fun and make Sir Winston laugh. How, I wasn't sure at that time. In the anteroom before the luncheon, I was told I would be sitting next to Britain's great wartime leader, and next to me on the other side would be the Maharaja of Baroda, who had recently lost his throne because of the changing order in India.

I noticed the Maharaja was laboriously scribbling notes on a large yellow tablet while aides hovered over him. I borrowed a few sheets of paper and started to scribble some of my own. I still didn't know what I was going to say until Danny walked into the room. I then made up my mind.

Just before Herbert, acting as toastmaster, got up to introduce me, the Maharaja, highly nervous, tore up his notes and started again. Inadvertently, he tore mine up as well. I had no time to scribble any more. Herbert was already making my introduction.

"Gentlemen," started Herbert, "I now bring you one of America's most distinguished speakers who is here to honor our guest today with a few words from America, the Toastmaster-General of the United States, Mr. George Jessel."

With Mr. and Mrs. Al Smith at the opening of "Little Old New York" at the 1939 World's Fair. From spending so much time with Al and Jimmy Walker, I can say now that what Smith and his party got away with in the New York of the thirties makes Watergate pale by comparison. The only difference was that Al didn't record his conversations.

(Above) Jimmy Walker, me, and Eddie Cantor, New York. (Below) With Harry Truman, Cardinal Cushing of Boston, and Police Commissioner Howard Fitzpatrick, Boston. (1956)

(Above) On an early morning stroll in New York with HST. I am admonishing a vociferous woman who had been heckling us. (New York Post Staff Photo) (Below) President John F. Kennedy, Averell Harriman, Mayor Robert Wagner of New York, during Jack's primary campaign for the presidency. (1958)

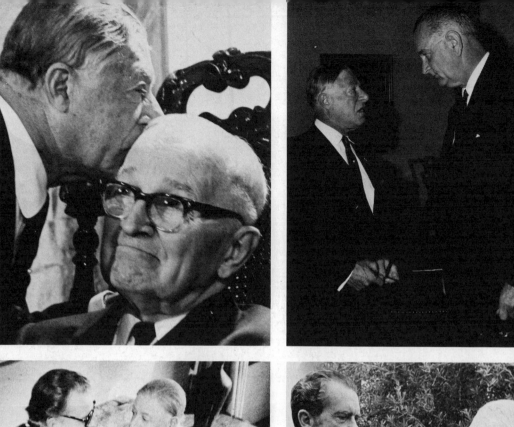

(Top left) Kissing HST goodnight after Los Angeles rally, 1948, when everyone but me had "kissed him off" in his election fight against Dewey. (Top right) With LBJ in the White House a few months after he succeeded JFK. The photo is inscribed, "To George Jessel, who has warmed the heart of America." (Bottom left) With Billy Graham, 1973. (Photo © 1973 by Michael S. Tomczyk) (Bottom right) With you know who, one of the great tragedies of American history. (Official White House Photo)

(Above) With former President Carlos Romulo of the Philippines. President Nixon was toying with the idea of naming me ambassador to the Philippines toward the end of his second term (which never arrived). (Below) With Scoop Jackson and his wife in Seattle in 1970.

(Above) At a luncheon in Los Angeles, 1951, with baseball managers (left to right) Fred Haney, Chuck Dressen, Leo Durocher, and Casey Stengel. (Below) At *that* Royal Command Performance: me, the Duchess of Kent, Johnny Ray, Queen Elizabeth, and producer Jack Hilton.

(Right) With Abba Eban,
Israel, 1970. (Below) With
David Ben Gurion, 1964.

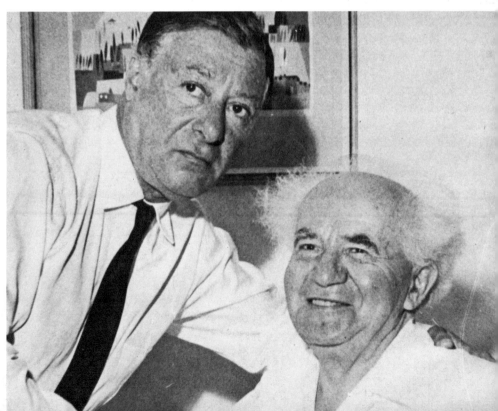

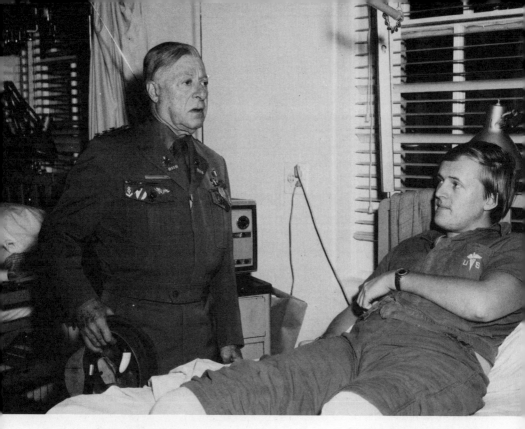

(Above) Visiting a GI in a hospital in Vietnam, 1970. (Left) One of my favorite pictures, taken while on a USO tour of Vietman.

I approached the podium and just as I got there I knew what I was going to do.

"Ladies and gentlemen, distinguished guests. I am highly complimented at the remarks of Mr. Herbert. I thought for a moment I was dead. (Nervous laughter.)

"But before attempting to amuse you today, or create a serious mood, may I say," and, at this, I turned and faced Sir Winston, "whatever dissension or discord that there might be between the United States and Great Britain, we are all fully in accord in our admiration for England's greatest man of the hour who saved this little Island and maybe the world."

Tears started to fill Sir Winston's eyes, and I never took mine off him as I continued.

"So, please, ladies and gentlemen, rise and let us drink a toast to the continued health of . . . Danny Kaye!"

The audience was stunned, until Sir Winston looked up at me and almost started to choke in his mirth. He nearly swallowed his cigar, and the rest of the audience then did just what I asked them to, including the Great Man himself. Two days later, I received a very warm note from Sir Winston and a huge box of Havana cigars. I still have the box. Danny never commented.

Before leaving for home, I flew to Scotland with Billy Graham to entertain some of our air force troops stationed in that northern outpost. Zsa Zsa Gabor also came along, and she and I were to meet again under strange circumstances several years later while I was making my last television show, "Here Come the Stars." But that comes later.

I would like to add here that the satisfaction of entertaining our troops overseas and visiting hospitals is a source of great satisfaction to me, and I have been doing it for many, many years. I mentioned earlier that benefits, even today, for some unknown individual or some unknown cause are the scourge of the theatrical profession. I have always told performers, young and old, that the best "benefits" are those of entertaining our armed forces around the world. It is far, far better to take a week or two of your time to do this rather than to attend obscure dinners for obscure people or causes so that the promoters of these events can line their pockets with a percentage of the take—a take made much higher when they can obtain, for free, the services of expensive talent who wouldn't think of doing a television appearance of even five minutes for less than $5,000. And yet, even today, I receive hundreds of requests to appear at benefits around the country, or for that matter, the world. I don't refer to testimonials, only benefits, which generally, in my experience, only "benefit" the promoters.

18

Four Loves Have I

EARLIER in this account of the world I lived in, I remarked that I made it a habit never to get laid in a beach house. Perhaps now is the time to explain my reasoning, because the beach house episode brought me my second daughter, of whom I am very fond.

After I returned from the Royal Command Performance, I immediately went on a cross-country tour for the United Jewish Appeal and helped to sell over one hundred million dollars in Bonds for Israel. This is a cause I have devoted many months out of the year to, off and on. I have also spent many weeks and many months touring army hospitals and army bases for the USO, interspersed with appearances on the "Tonight" show, with both Johnny Carson and Jack Paar, as well as others of its ilk. I was never idle for a moment following my exit from Fox.

When I first met Joan Tyler in Hollywood I was "between appearances," and she was a struggling young actress and an extraordinarily beautiful young lady. We fell in love and became engaged to be married. She never told me that she was also engaged at the same time to a wealthy Mexican businessman, Tony Ruffo, whom she married after we broke up. But my involvement with

Joan was to have disastrous financial consequences for me five
years later.

During our "engagement," I had to make another tour of the
U.S. Army bases in Germany and England, and I took Joan along
with me for a semi-vacation. She never became pregnant during all
that time. We both contracted a bad virus, and then I contracted a
bad cold on my return to California. Because of my serious reaction to it, Joan told the press she couldn't see spending the rest of
her life with me. While she didn't say it at the time, she felt I was
"too old for her." She also complained of my constant traveling
"here, there, and everywhere" and feared that it would interfere
with her career. She then married Ruffo even though she claimed
to be in love with me.

While we were only engaged for several months, we always
remained friendly, and whenever she came to California, Joan always called me to say hello if I were in town. In 1960 I had leased a
beach house at Santa Monica quite near Norma's old mansion. I
returned home from a dinner engagement one evening, and as my
driver pulled up to the front door, I saw Joan sitting on the door-
step waiting for me.

After she got inside, she told me she had broken up with Ruffo
and planned to divorce him. She also added that she had nowhere
to stay and that she had left her three-year-old daughter by Ruffo
with friends for the night. Naturally, after a few belts, I asked her
to spend the night with me.

We just spent that one night together, and I didn't see her
anymore, romantically speaking, although she did telephone me
several times during the next few weeks.

I had known the former maverick mayor of Los Angeles, Sam
Yorty, for many years—just as I had been very friendly with another maverick, James J. Walker. When Sam was re-elected for a
second term, he asked me to make the introductory speech at his
inaugural on July 1, 1961, on the steps of the Los Angeles City Hall.
Just as I finished and had introduced Sam, a man made his way
through the mob of well-wishers and came up to me.

"Mr. Jessel? May I talk to you for a moment?"

Before I could reply, he stuffed some papers in my hand.

"See you in court," and he high-tailed it through the crowd
before I could even swear at him.

When I looked at the papers he had handed me, I discovered it was a subpoena to answer a paternity suit filed by Joan the previous day. She was claiming I was the father of her unborn child. In the suit she asked for $2,050 medical expenses, $750 per month support during her pregnancy, and $960 per month after the child was born. Naturally, at sixty-three, I was flattered to even be considered a father again. I decided to fight the suit because she had only just left her husband the night before she was with me at the beach house.

Actually, one night during May, Joan had called me about three in the morning to tell me she "thought" she was pregnant but wasn't sure. I discussed an amicable settlement, half-jokingly, with her at the time. I didn't believe it and thought she was using it as an excuse to get me to break up with another tempestuous love —Marjorie Morgan with whom I was having an affair at the time. (More about that episode later on.)

I discussed it with one of my attorneys, and we decided to fight the suit, which eventually cost me, with attorneys' fees and support, a great deal of money. I went through blood and semen tests; the nurse in the doctor's office had to aid me in the latter, but that was something that had to be accomplished as part of the preliminary court orders and her duty as a nurse.

(Under a strange California law, the judge in a paternity suit can decide parentage if a suspected or alleged father refuses to make himself available for such blood and semen tests. They are never positive, per se, but only establish the fact that a man *could* be the father of a child having the same groupings.)

On December 27, 1961, Charis Carla (Jessel) was born. The case finally came to trial and the judge ruled that I was the father of the child. I could think of nothing else to say to the judge, but: "Your honor, I want to thank you for this compliment. I will, at my advanced age, accept your decision with pride. . . ."

When I toted up the legal bills, support and medical expenses I was ordered to pay, that one night at my beach house cost me over $200,000. That is why I have made it a rule never to get laid in a beach house for the past twelve years or more.

Immediately after I stopped dating Joan in 1957, I had a very nice fling with Rita Hayworth, one of my favorite people. During the eleven years I was producing pictures for Darryl and 20th

Century-Fox, I had dated Rita several times, escorting her to a lot of industry affairs.

She telephoned me one day between trips for the UJA and asked if I would escort her to the premiere of some film or other. Naturally, I was only too delighted. This resulted in our steady dating again over a period of two or three months. Our pictures, while we were out together, appeared in newspapers and magazines from London to Cape Town, and New York to Los Angeles. Many gossip columnists, such as Louella Parsons, Winchell, Hopper, and others, came out with statements that Rita and I were "engaged."

While dining at Ciros one night, we had both imbibed a great deal of sauce, and while we were dancing, I asked Rita to marry me. I have had a penchant for asking young ladies this question, but, thank God, I have only been caught three times—none of which I regret. My batting average in the other respect, as you no doubt have gathered, is far, far higher. Anyway, Rita and I both decided we couldn't make liars out of the gossips of Hollywood.

She agreed enthusiastically, and we climbed into the back seat of my car for the trip to Las Vegas. Because of the effect of the booze, we fell asleep while George, my chauffeur of many years, started out on the seven-hour drive to Baghdad-on-the-Desert. At Baker, George stopped for gas. It was then that Rita woke up; her head was in my lap, face up. She stretched, looked up at me, and murmured, "I love you, Phil!"

With that, I shouted to George: "Back to Los Angeles. . . ."

Many years later, Rita and I laughed about that night and she said she had never dated anyone she could remember named "Phil," let alone been in love with such a person. She doesn't know to this day who "Phil" could have been, or who she was thinking (or dreaming?) about.

More's the pity. . . for "Phil."

In 1961, just before the paternity suit, I was embroiled in a very stormy, tempestuous affair with Marjorie Morgan * of whom Joan was very jealous even though she was married to another man at the time.

My publicist and friend for many years, Stanley Cowan, had

---

* Not her real name. And when you read this you'll know why. She's a tiger.

put together a promotion with the Matson Lines for something they called "Sail with the Stars," wherein personalities would sail on the *Lurline* and *Matsonia* to Honolulu and give two shows during the five-day voyage, generally the second and fourth nights at sea. There was great competition with the airlines and Matson was doing everything to attract passengers to Honolulu.

Cowan and his girl—he was between marriages at the time—myself and Marjorie, Ben Oakland and his performer-wife, a dance team, and a male singer made arrangements for the trip.

Stanley, through Hawaiian columnist Eddie Sherman, had also arranged for us to play a couple of NCO and officers' clubs on the island at a good fee. (This had nothing to do with my gratis USO trips. The NCO and officers' clubs still hire talent from the States.) This is the reason I took along the extra performers.

Marjorie and I did not share a room on the boat going over, but she had a cabin across the passageway—if that is the correct nautical term. I became so disgusted with her tantrums during the voyage—she wanted to go off on her own all the time—I even asked Stanley to see if he could arrange for a helicopter from the mainland to take her off and fly her back to Los Angeles. This was so impractical, according to Cowan, I dropped the idea. We continued the voyage under an armed truce, so to speak.

We were all booked into the Royal Hawaiian Hotel with Marjorie and myself in a huge suite with two bedrooms—one on either side of the living room. Marjorie was in one bedroom, I in the other; this was part of the animosity between us from the day we left Wilmington. I also had along my trusty pistol and plenty of ammunition.

Eddie Sherman had also booked us into the main room of the Royal Hawaiian for a good fee—fifty percent of the admissions. We did the shows as per schedule, but following the second night's show, Marjorie did not come back to the room. I didn't know where she'd gone. (I was told later she had made out with one of the naval officers attending the show.) I started hitting the bottle, and by 6:00 A.M., I had emptied almost two fifths of bourbon and called the Honolulu Police Department and reported her as missing.

At 6:30, I decided to call Stanley in his room six doors down the hall and tell him what I had done. In the meantime, I had put my trusty pistol and the ammunition on the bed in my bedroom, packed all of Marjorie's things in her five suitcases—enough for an African safari instead of a week's trip to Hawaii—and stacked them in the foyer of the suite. A few minutes later Stan came plodding half asleep down the hall in his bathrobe. He promptly proceeded to fall over her luggage. No one in our business is awake at six-thirty in the morning with one exception—me.

I told Stanley what I had done and he blew his stack.

"Good God, Georgie, it will be in all the newspapers. What the hell did you call the cops for?"

I never got a chance to tell him because just at that moment the telephone rang. It was the desk clerk to advise me that the Honolulu P.D. was downstairs and would like to talk to me. I sent Stanley down to try to smooth things over. As a press agent of long standing, he had had plenty of experience in such matters.

Nevertheless, the police insisted on coming up to the room to see if I was all right. In the meantime, Marjorie came sauntering back to the suite, saw her suitcases in the foyer, and let out with a stream of four-letter words not even I had heard before, and damn few longshoremen, either.

"No son of a bitch can put me out of my room," was one of her milder phrases as the police and Stan walked in. When I explained to them that Marjorie had come home, and that everything was all right, they left. Luckily, Marjorie kept her mouth shut or they would have hauled her in for assaulting the English language.

But then all hell broke loose, and Marjorie came storming out of her room throwing everything at me she could find. I was dressed in Bermuda shorts and a beret, and the damn shorts kept falling down. I had an insane desire to keep the beret intact, to hell with the shorts. I didn't know which to grab first. I picked up a chair, ready to throw it at her, when Stanley put his arm in the way and deflected it, almost breaking his wrist in the process. Then I passed out on the couch. Under the circumstances, Stan thought I had had a heart attack.

He sent Marjorie out of the suite and called the nurse—there was no house doctor on call so early. After checking my pulse, she decided, after seeing the two almost empty bottles, that I had merely passed out. She gave me a shot to knock me out for eight hours—or so she thought.

Stanley then, he told me later, walked into the bedroom and saw the gun on the bed. He, too, almost passed out, but picked up the weapon, put it in his pocket, and took it downstairs, still in his bathrobe. He asked the manager to put it in the safe and to surrender it to no one but him when we were ready to leave. I'm glad he found it and not me, because in my hazy state, like the Norma Talmadge–Carvel James episode in Palm Beach many years before, I would have started shooting, probably killed Marjorie, Stan, myself, and anybody else who had stood in the way.

When I came downstairs around twelve, after a four-hour "nap," I asked Stanley and Benny Oakland if I had caused any problems during the night. I couldn't remember a damn thing.

"No, Georgie," said Stanley, laughing. "It's all squared away now."

"Yeah, but some son of a bitch stole my pistol and I better call the police!"

It was then that Stanley told me what had happened and what he had done with the gun.

Thank God he did, or there could have been disaster. Marjorie took the next flight back. I had to be in New York for the Jack Paar show on Monday. Meanwhile, Stanley had checked around to see if we could do anything to entertain the garrison in Honolulu on Saturday night. As long as we were there, we felt we could put on a show for them.

The navy jumped at the chance and arranged for us to perform at Pearl Harbor. They didn't tell us that it would be on a flat top with over 5,000 people watching us. Because of the conditions, the enthusiasm, the brass and servicemen sitting on that flight deck, I put on one of the best shows I had ever done. Everything was just right—the sound system was the best I had ever used, and the audience the most enthusiastic. Following the show, we had a motorcycle escort to a reception at the home of General Hap Arnold. In spite of the Marjorie Morgan episode, it turned out to be an excellent sojourn.

While we are on the subject of my latter-day romances, I may as well continue. Not only did I mention earlier that I would never get laid in a beach house, but I also made a reference to the fact that I had to have a little romance before I got laid. This has held true with one exception—Xaviera Hollander.

In the spring of 1970, I was in New York and having dinner at the Golden Key Chinese restaurant with Mac and Bob Kriendler, the owners of Manhattan's famed Twenty-One. (You don't have to say their own place was too expensive even for them, they just wanted a change of pace!)

Halfway through the meal, the head waiter came over to me with a sheepish grin on his normally inscrutable countenance.

"Mr. Jessel, there is a young lady in the lobby who would like to have a few words with you."

"Is she pretty?" I asked him.

"Oh, very, Mr. Jessel, and she's quite well known."

I walked out into the lobby and saw a tall, beautiful blonde standing there with a copy of a book under her arm. She came up to me with a big smile on her face. "Mr. Jessel, I have always loved your work, and I would like you to have a copy of the book I have just written, *The Happy Hooker*."

I realized immediately that this very pretty, well-built young lady, with a figure like the proverbial outhouse, was Xaviera Hollander, New York's most famous latter-day madam and practitioner of the world's oldest profession. After chatting with her for a few minutes, I suggested we have dinner the next evening and get to know each other. I knew it wouldn't take much "romancing" to get me into bed with this one, even though I first discovered my idiosyncrasy in New Orleans four decades before.

On our second date, I found myself in her apartment and being taught a few things I had never known before, even with my experience. But I must admit it was very disconcerting when, several times while we were engaged in sexual acrobatics on her king-sized bed, the telephone would ring and Xaviera would disappear for upwards of an hour at a time. She left me laying there—you will pardon the ungrammatical expression under the circumstances—wondering whether or not the joint was going to be raided and she'd taken off for the hills. Unfortunately, Xaviera was undergoing deportation hearings at the time. All Xaviera ever said during these absences was, "Wait for me, darling . . . I'll be back in a little while. . . ."

The third time it happened, I asked her about it.

"Darling, just remember, sex is business with me, except for those I like. I have to see these very old clients when they call. But you are my romance of the hour, so please don't even think about it. It's pleasure with you, not business!"

At least she didn't bring them home with her while I was there. I suppose she believed in the old cliche, "Let's go to your place and let your mother worry!"

Xaviera and I went together for three wildly romantic and sexually acrobatic weeks, and then I had to leave for a Caribbean cruise on another "Sail with the Stars" promotion and a boatload of junketeering plumbers and their wives, or some such group.

But I must add here that Xaviera is a sparkling woman to be with even though she was the most notorious and controversial madam in New York's recent history. A Dutch Jewess, she speaks six languages, is a brilliant conversationalist, and the most gifted woman in a bedroom I have ever experienced.

It is, I think, worth pointing out here in context, that I was cancelled for the first time in my life for something I said while on that cruise. Russia has always frightened me, and I loathe and detest their treatment of the Russian Jews. What I said then, I meant, and I still mean it.

On these cruises I usually did a half-hour act, but one night I did about an hour because the audience was warm and in a good mood, so I just kept going. I then went down into the audience and sat at several of the tables; naturally, I had a few snorts at each one.

Finally, they insisted I stay on stage a little longer. Unfortunately, I did. At the end of a few songs, I concluded:

"I have nothing left to do, ladies and gentlemen, but I would like to leave you with something very profound for you to remember me by. In fact, it is far more important than my songs and jokes. Simply, it is:

"Fuck mother Russia."

I was immediately cancelled by the captain of the ship, put ashore in Puerto Rico, sort of a modern-day walking the plank, and went home to California. I don't think the cruise line out of Miami is still in business.

19

Two Presidents, the Press, and Pumpernickel

As I stated earlier, of all the presidents since Calvin Coolidge the only one I did not become friends with, or have a passing acquaintance of, was General Eisenhower.

I only met him once very briefly in the receiving line at a state dinner. I found him, in those few seconds, to be very charming but very aloof. However, from other friends in government, including Lyndon B. Johnson, I was told that Ike didn't really run the country; John Foster Dulles did. Ike was considered by his cabinet as the Chairman of the Board who believed in relegating responsibility. Unfortunately, Dulles did not like me, nor anyone who looked like me or who had my religious heritage.

Most people I know, in or out of government, considered the late John Foster Dulles a terrible bigot and very anti-Jew; not anti-Semitic, but anti-Jew. To my knowledge, Dulles never set foot in the state of Israel the entire time he was secretary of state although his government had always supported Israel from the days of Harry S. Truman. His friends told me that he became anti-Jew after he ran against Governor Herbert Lehman for the senate in New York and was defeated by the vote of the Jewish population of

182

New York City. That did something to him, apparently, and he hated everyone who ever set foot in a synagogue, or was of the Jewish religion.

Lyndon Johnson and I were very close. I think I visited him at least twenty or thirty times during the time he was vice-president and the president. Several times when I was sitting in his offices, I heard Lyndon on the telephone, and I can tell you here and now that if you think the "deleted expletives" in the Watergate tapes were raunchy, you should have heard Lyndon on the telephone to his cronies and cabinet members. He could come out with some four-letter words and phrases I had never heard before.

I have always been very grateful to Lyndon for what he did for Eddie Cantor. While John F. Kennedy was in office, I proposed that the government award Eddie, with the consent of Congress, the Medal of Freedom for all the philanthropic work he had done during his lifetime. Eddie's life was slipping away, and I felt such an honor would do him good. Unfortunately, JFK was assassinated before he could put this before Congress, although it was in the works. I called Lyndon about this, and in his own bulldozing way with the Congress, he got this through in record-breaking time. Former Governor Edmond G. Brown (Sr.) of California and I presented this to Eddie on the lawn of his Beverly Hills home. He was far too ill to go to Washington to receive it. Stanley Cowan called the Los Angeles papers and the three television networks to attend the presentation. We did not want a huge mob because of Eddie's health. As it turned out, word got around and every photographer, reporter, and television and radio station in and around Los Angeles had people there—it was a mob scene. Eddie loved it, although he was just not strong enough to say too much. He was very grateful, but unfortunately, he died several months later. I have always been very appreciative of Lyndon's efforts on Eddie's behalf.

Many people, at my speaking engagements, have asked me the past two years, what I thought about Richard Nixon. What can one say about a friend of many years' standing? Suffice it to say that the story of Richard Nixon shows what a great country this is—and it is the best story you can tell about this great country of ours and the opportunity it presents to all its citizens. After Nixon was defeated for the governorship of California in 1962, nobody gave him a chance to ever run for public office again. You could have gotten Las Vegas odds of ten to one that Nixon couldn't have been elected doorman at Twenty-One. But he did come back to narrowly defeat Senator Humphrey and win re-election over Senator McGovern by one of the largest pluralities in the history of the country.

But I did feel something was wrong with Nixon three or so years ago when he held a huge garden party at the Western White House in San Clemente. Present were all the top names of show business from New York to Hollywood. Also present, though, were top members of his government, including Henry Kissinger, John Mitchell—before the Water Closet case broke—practically every member of the cabinet and several ambassadors.

I will never forget the scene; it was a beautiful summer day and the Pacific Ocean was shimmering in the background. The roses in Pat Nixon's garden were never more beautiful and the green grass surrounding La Casa Pacifica was putting-green perfect. The wives, mistresses, and girl friends of those present were dressed as if for a tea party at Buckingham Palace.

Lined up in front of the president in a semicircle waiting for him to address the assembled throng, we all stood and waited for him to begin. In the front row were Kissinger, Mitchell, the cabinet members and the ambassadors. Myself, Sammy Davis, Jack Benny, Frank Sinatra, George Burns, and every other star you could think of were behind them.

Nixon approached the microphones. "I would like to welcome all of you here today," said the then president. "I would also like to say that if my father were alive today, the one thing he would be most proud of was that I numbered among my close friends, Jack Benny!"

A deathly hush fell over the group before a scattered round of applause greeted his remarks. I was stunned that he had slighted so many other important and world-famous people such as Henry Kissinger. So was everyone else.

I mentioned earlier that I felt the press held a hate relationship with Richard Nixon all through the years since the Helen Gahagan Douglas senatorial campaign of 1950. I would like to expand on that here in context if I may.

Helen Douglas happened to be a Roman Catholic and married to a half-Jew by the name of Melvyn Douglas. As it has been stated many times by more profound minds than mine, all is fair in love, war, and politics, and Nixon was told many times by his advisers that as Southern California, where he would have to draw most of his voter strength, was so heavily Democratic in registration, he would have to go on the attack in order to be elected.

I have checked and rechecked the campaign rhetoric of that campaign, and I can definitely state here and now that Nixon never called Helen Gahagan Douglas "a communist," as the liberal press has constantly charged him with. He did call her a "pinko," which is far different from calling her a communist.

The press, over the intervening twenty years, has twisted this around so much—and if you repeat a lie often enough, it is bound to be believed—that he has always been accused of this. It is very unfair. Just as it is unfair not to mention that the General Services Administration spent many millions on the LBJ Ranch in Texas while LBJ was vice-president and president. But when Richard Nixon does it, it is made out to be a crime—fraud at the very least.

I, myself, have had a sample or two of how the press, in this case the electronic press, treats those who disagree with their liberal views. In fact, my case was very well publicized in 1971.

On my return from a tour of U. S. military bases in Spain, England, and Germany, I was asked to go on the "Today" show on NBC and be interviewed by Edwin Newman, a substitute host for the week.

I described the morale of the U.S. Armed Forces in Europe, in response to a Newman question, as "very high." But I did add: "But, of course, when you pick up a copy of *Pravda*, excuse me, the *New York Times*, you generally see all negative reporting. Dope raids, dope usage, murders, and killings. The *Times* and the *Washington Post*, excuse me, *Pravda* number two, take a very anti-American, negative attitude—both of these papers."

The reason I came out with this was that, just before I left for Madrid, I had been on an annual one-night stand tour for entrepreneur Roy Radin, who puts on annual shows throughout the east for the Firemen and Policemen's Benevolent Associations. I have done this tour every year for five years. I finished the tour in Boston and left directly for Spain. The weather was beautiful, the sun was shining, the sky was blue, the children were swimming in lakes, ponds, and swimming pools.

When I arrived in Madrid, a newspaperman who met me asked, "Didn't you just arrive from Boston, Mr. Jessel?"

"Yes," I replied, wondering what was coming next.

His next question made me wonder even more. "Is anyone still alive in New England?"

I immediately conjectured that there had been a terrible catastrophe in New England while I was over the Atlantic. "What the hell do you mean, 'Is anyone still alive?'" I answered him.

He then showed me a copy of the *New York Times* with a headline, "Hundreds Dying of Smog and Pollution in New England." Nobody I had seen in New England even had a cough.

When Newman asked me what I meant by calling the *Times* and the *Post* "Pravda," I tried to tell him this same story.

But he broke in very upset. "You are a guest here, Mr. Jessel, but I don't really think very much of this talk about '*Pravda*, excuse me, the *New York Times*; *Pravda*, excuse me, the *Washington Post*.' I think what you're saying, if you mean it, is very serious. . . ."

I replied that I didn't mean it that way, and the engineers were signaling frantically for Newman to break for a commercial. The interview had been scheduled for six minutes and lasted less than three.

I would like to say that I do not believe that Newman was entirely at fault in this incident. During the commercial break, he received a call on the set from the producer's Ivory Tower and was told he didn't want to hear anymore about the *New York Times* or *Washington Post*. This was from the same man who had written a book, in conjunction with his father or brother, or some other relative, about what a great man Muhammad Ali was because he refused to be inducted into the armed forces on a technicality. He gave credit to Ali for standing up for his rights, but he barred me from freedom of speech on his program because I didn't agree with *his* views.

I learned later, also, that Newman told Abel Green, editor of *Variety*, the show business weekly, that he had "orders" to get me off the air during the commercial break. But it is very interesting that I haven't been allowed on network television since that time.

Prior to this incident, and for many years before, I had been on the Jack Paar version of the "Tonight Show" at least fifty or sixty times. I had been on with Carson a like number of times when he was in New York and after he moved to California. I can say I was on the "Tonight Show" on the average of every six weeks or less.

When I called the producer of the show, Freddie de Cordova, he told me: "Don't call me about it, George. There's too much opposition to you from the network. Just forget about appearing on the 'Tonight Show' anymore."

Before I finish my views on this subject, I do believe the press of the country, electronic, print, and spoken, is far too negative. Just pick up the sports pages, as an example, and you will see what I mean. Generally, nine times out of ten, you will read "Pirates Lose." Very seldom will you see "Dodgers Win." There can be one little patch of smog in a certain area, and you are bound to read such a headline as that which appeared in the issue of the *New York Times* to which I referred. It is *negative* reporting whichever way you look at it. It is, to my mind, a hell of an attitude, and it places the country in a bad light around the world. I have used this as a theme for many of my hundreds of luncheon and dinner speaking engagements around the country, and the audiences, on the whole, have agreed with me.

I have made a very good living the past several years, receiving upwards of $2,500 for each appearance. My income has never been less than $100,000 a year—generally a lot more. Apropos of this, two or three years ago, to show you what the press can do to you, the *National Enquirer* came out with a story headlined, "George Jessel Is Broke." This could not be further from the truth.

What the story didn't say following the interview was that, compared to Jack Benny, Milton Berle, George Burns, Jimmy Durante, and Eddie Cantor, and others of my ilk, I am certainly not a millionaire in the sense that they are. People tend to forget that Hope, Burns, Benny, and the rest of them had tremendous weekly salaries from their radio and television shows for as long as twenty or thirty years without a break. I never had any of these long runs on radio or television, and they managed to accumulate most of their wealth before very high income taxes came into effect.

The offshoot of that *Enquirer* story was that several weeks later I received an offer from an oil company executive in Ohio asking me if I would be interested in "fronting" for them in a public relations capacity for a very good salary. Even though the offer was appreciated, the *entire* story was *not* told in the *Enquirer*; again, negative reporting to sell papers.

Apart from my speaking engagements, and a few appearances on the "Merv Griffin Show"—which is not network—I have also done a couple of films. For one of these I spent seven weeks on the island of Malta in the Mediterranean with Milton Berle, Anthony Newley and his wife Joan Collins, and several others.

The picture was *Hieronymous Merkin*,—it had a longer title than that but is best forgotten—and I played the role of "Dr. Death," dressed in a white suit, and had to follow Tony Newley around all through the picture. The film was a fantasy that died at the box office, although it did receive a lot of publicity including a three- or four-page color layout in *Playboy*.

Quite frankly, following that film, I came to realize what a tremendous egotist Newley is. He has the biggest ego in show business. For example, what other actor would strut around in the nude in front of his children in a film? Both of his children by Joan Collins had roles in the picture, and it was a *tour de force* for Newley. Joan had a cameo role. I enjoyed myself with Berle because we sat on the set all day playing cards. I also realized what a fine dramatic actor Milton is when he puts his mind to it. (In case I haven't mentioned it before, Milton was born next door to me on 118th Street ten years after I first saw the light of day.)

I also had a small part in an Orson Welles film that started shooting three or four years ago in Paris and hasn't been released at the time this was written. I have tried to reach Orson several times in London, Rome, Paris, and Vienna but have never been able to catch up with him to find out even the title of the film. I expect it will show up one of these days.

One of my biggest disappointments and heartaches the past several years has been over the way the Friars Club of California has treated me. As I told you earlier, Bing Crosby and I founded the California version in the late forties, even though Bing never set foot in the place after that. They have completely ignored me the past several years even though I lunch or dine there several times a week when I am home.

Most of you are probably aware of the fact that I originated the roasts of show business celebrities at the New York Friars Club many years ago. I have not, in recent years, been asked to attend or speak at any of these roasts at the Friars. Dean Martin started doing them on his regular weekly show, and then as a special now and again since his cancellation. Kraft Cheese also sponsored several of them as specials on one of the three networks. I was never mentioned in any of them. I suppose it is Madison Avenue's fault again.

In 1968, Four Star-International contracted me for twenty-six of these roasts under the title "Here Come the Stars," which were syndicated very successfully. We had some of the top stars in show business on the show—as the subjects and as guests.

It was during the filming—or taping, rather—of one of the shows that Zsa Zsa Gabor and I had our well-publicized run-in when she showed up almost two hours late for one taping session.

Two shows were to be taped that day, and Zsa Zsa was to appear as a guest on the first one, with Art Linkletter to be roasted on the second. Four Star had rented expensive studio space at NBC in Burbank, with an entire crew standing by with their fingers up their asses waiting for Madame Zsa Zsa to show up on the set. The then Los Angeles District Attorney Evelle Younger was also present to appear on the Linkletter roast.

Zsa Zsa arrived a little after one-thirty—she was due at noon ready to go on. She then demanded the services of a manicurist and time to have her hair done. She had arrived in rollers and ermine, and with a hairdresser in tow. She then imperiously demanded to be served with a cream cheese sandwich on pumpernickel bread. I doubt if very many of you have ever eaten at the NBC commissary in Burbank. At that time it was in the back of two catering trucks parked in the alley. You would be extremely fortunate to get cream cheese at all, let alone pumpernickel at any hour of the day. What you did manage to find, you ate out of a can or a carton and unwrapped cellophane from the sandwiches.

I was called to the dressing room to see what I could do with

Miss Gabor—and then it started. Zsa Zsa refused to budge her well-publicized ass from the makeup chair until her nails had been manicured and she had her sandwich delivered. This was all too much for me because I am a professional, always have been, and always will be. When I am due somewhere at a certain time, I am always there five minutes early—socially or professionally. I should also add that all the other stars, who appeared on "Here Come the Stars" for scale, always showed up on time and ready to go in front of the cameras.

Zsa Zsa let loose with some Hungarian expletives, which I understood but would not print in this book; they were just too raunchy. Even my ancestral lineage was questioned and I retaliated. Len Miller, the associate producer, Stanley Cowan, Dave Charnay, president of Four Star, and everyone else involved were trying to smooth things over, but to no avail. The time was rapidly approaching to start the taping of the second show, and we were paying $10,000 or more for each hour we weren't utilizing the studio.

Even Evelle Younger, now the California attorney-general, made an appearance in the small makeup room to see what the fracas was about. I heard someone say to him, "I bet you didn't know television was so exciting, did you, Mr. Younger?" Evelle just shook his head, turned on his well-polished heel, and walked back to the green room. Someone else commented that it was like the second-act curtain of *The Man Who Came to Dinner*.

Zsa Zsa then decided to call the *gendarmes* because of the animosity she had created, and departed loudly declaring she would bring suit against me. To top everything else off, she even demanded $10,000 to "buy this dollink boy a pair of cufflinks he wants." That was a reference to the swishy hairdresser she brought with her. He was having conniption fits at the row and was hissing "Dear me's" all over the studio.

Cowan started to worry because a little white line started to show on my upper lip and he felt I was going to have a heart attack. I also broke out in a cold sweat, usually another indication of heart problems. Luckily I did not.

"Let her go," I yelled as the Burbank police and NBC security people arrived. "I'm used to working with responsible artists and not a broad like this. We're going to tape this show if it's the last thing I do. I hope she does sue me. I'd like to get that Hungarian bitch in court.''

On her way out, Zsa Zsa added that she would sue Four Star, NBC, the commissary, and everyone else in the place as well. We only taped one show that day and had to make up for the lost time the following week at a staggering cost.

But let me illustrate the mentality of Zsa Zsa Gabor one step further. It happened a few years before the Four Star incident. We were both guests at a private dinner party, and Zsa Zsa heard that I was going to London—I believe it was for the Command Performance—and she asked me at which hotel I was going to stay.

"The Savoy, as usual," I told her.

"Dollink, don't be silly. Why don't you stay as my guest at Buckingham Palace? I just bought it from the Queen.''

I don't think she was kidding, either. In my opinion, her delusions of majestic grandeur honestly had her believing that she *had* bought the Palace.

Poor Zsa Zsa.

As to my latter-day romances, only two are worth mentioning. One was well publicized, the other not so well because nothing spectacular happened and the young lady was well into her thirties. This one, like the Marjorie Morgan incident, also ended up on an unfortunate note. It seems Honolulu has a jinx on me, particularly my lady friends.

I went steadily with Tina Grace for three years, or a little longer. "Tina Grace" is not her real name because she is now happily married, the mother of two young children, and a pillar of her community.

An agent had put together an appearance for me at the Honolulu International Convention Center with a small show I brought from the mainland. The show had been ballyhooed for several weeks and a sellout was anticipated. The auditorium in which I was to appear was the HICC stadium complex, a small Madison Square Garden.

Four hours before we were to open on the first night, the heavens opened up with the biggest rainstorm I had ever seen in my life. Instead of the 5,000 people or more to whom they had sold tickets, only 2,000 showed up. For the first two or three days we had nothing but rain starting about 4:30 each afternoon like clockwork.

Stanley Cowan and his bride came along on a delayed honeymoon, and I brought Tina with me as she felt like a vacation. Also, I hate to be alone on trips of more than two days. I get very lonely. I couldn't expect Stanley and his bride to spend all their time with me; they were on their honeymoon. I was looking forward to a wonderful week or ten days with Tina. We had a beautiful suite at the Royal Hawaiian, just a few doors down the hall from the one I had occupied with Marjorie a few years before.

The days were beautiful—sunny, hot, and with a trade wind blowing so that it never became uncomfortable. But, like clockwork every afternoon for four days at 4:30, the heavens opened up.

On the second day Tina rented a surfboard and floated out to sea, and the silly girl fell asleep in the fierce sun. She had never been to Hawaii before and didn't realize how treacherous the sun could be. Stanley, myself, and his bride, lay on the beach relaxing. Within one hour Tina was burned to a crisp—so much so we asked the beach attendant to call a doctor. None of us dared touch her after she had paddled back to shore. After taking one look at her, the doctor asked two of the attendants to carry her up to the suite on a stretcher.

"This young lady has a very bad case of third-degree sunburn, Mr. Jessel," were the doctor's first words after examining Tina. "She has to stay in bed for at least three or four days, and then she may be able to get up and then be very careful. She will probably have to use crutches for two or three weeks after that."

On the sixth day, Tina was still in such pain she couldn't even get out of bed comfortably to go to the bathroom. There was only one thing to do. I asked Stanley to arrange for her to return to the mainland and spend a few weeks at my house in the valley, as I had to leave Hawaii and go straight to New York for an appearance on the "Tonight Show" and the "Merv Griffin Show." As it turned out, Tina was out of commission for three weeks and then could only walk very painfully on crutches for another week after that.

Unfortunately, Tina was always asking for things such as negligees, jewelry, and other adornments. I have always liked to do things for my lady loves, and to buy them pretty things without their asking for everything. I enjoyed Tina's company and she mine. While I was in Chicago for a speaking engagement for two or three days, she met her present husband and I wished her well. But I must say here and now that it was a pleasant three years.

I should add here that, after the fourth day, the rains stopped in Honolulu and we closed to SRO houses and a very successful engagement. But after the two incidents on the islands—with Tina and with Marjorie—I have never been back there.

Following the Tina Grace affair, I met Audrey McGee in Midland, Texas, where I was to address a cattlemen's convention. She had recently filed for divorce from her husband and I flipped over her. I brought Audrey to Hollywood, and, as I was signed to do a picture with Bill Castle at Paramount, I asked him to test Audrey for the role of my wife, Mrs. Fessel, in a turkey called *The Busy Bodies*. It was a macabre sort of film wherein bodies kept disappearing from a mortuary. It eventually showed up as the late movie on television—only once.

I was really in love with Audrey and wanted to marry her. I presented her with an engagement ring on the set of *The Busy Bodies*—with appropriate press coverage—and we planned to be married immediately following the *Hieronymous Merkin* picture in Malta; she was to meet me in Rome for the ceremony. I was constantly buying her little trinkets to which, to her everlasting credit, she strenuously objected. Audrey, twenty-four when I first met her, told the press at the "engagement party," "Shall we say George is sixty-eight going on twenty-one? He has more energy than I have. . . ."

While I was in Malta, Audrey went back to her husband and never showed up in Rome. I spent a fortune in trans-Atlantic telephone calls from the Holy City before I finally located her in Texas and she told me what had happened.

When I fall, I fall hard, and as I have said many times, like a lot of other men, I would prefer to play the balcony scene than make a bank deposit!

Life is more fun that way.

20

Curtain Call

Iᴛ seems I never learn, particularly with regard to the stock market following my almost half-million-dollar losses in the crash of '29. All during the time I was with 20th Century-Fox, I started buying stocks again—blue chip stuff, not the junk I used to buy. I had over $400,000 invested when the mini-crash of '62 hit the country during the Kennedy regime. In two days I had lost, on paper, over $200,000 and more each day.

One evening Stanley Cowan and I were sitting in the Luau in Beverly Hills having an evening bracer when in walked my stock broker, whom I hadn't been able to reach for several days. I gave him hell for not returning my calls and for advising me to buy the stuff I did. I blamed everything on him—not the economic conditions that caused the slump.

"Sell everything I own," I ordered him. "Salvage what you can and I'll buy a whorehouse in Hong Kong. It's more profitable."

"Just hang on, George," he advised, playing with my money. "They'll come up again. It's only a temporary slump."

He said he would see about it and walked out. I'm glad he did because the market suddenly started to climb again.

194

A few weeks later Stanley and I were again in the Luau and the broker walked in with a big grin on his face and threw some papers on the table in front of me.

"Now see why I didn't sell everything? Instead of losing over $200,000, you've not only gotten it back, you've made an additional $30,000." I bought him a drink, and I never did get around to buying that whorehouse—although I did sell out a few months later.

But, as you have no doubt surmised, my life has been full of ups and downs for the past seventy-odd years, and I wouldn't have traded it for any other.

I have met many fine people during that time and made and formed close, long-lasting friendships with many of them. I have been fortunate indeed to be on a first-name basis with presidents, kings, gangsters, and the biggest names in show business. I treasure every one of those friendships; I have never presumed on any of them, and that is the only way to maintain friendships over the years. I have been stone broke and down to my last cigar, but very, very few people ever knew it. Only my closest associates and my attorneys—and my ex-wives. That is the way it should be.

Space has precluded me from talking about many of these people in the preceding pages. I have no wish to slight any of them, so perhaps a capsule mention of my feelings toward them—particularly those in show business (many of them dead)—will clear my conscience for not mentioning them in greater detail and my association with them over the years. My era of show business has been, perhaps, the most productive of any era of America. More stars were born during my seven decades than ever before. Unfortunately, we no longer have Jack Benny, Fred Allen, Joe E. Lewis, and so many other fine performers with us to brighten our lives and those of the people they entertained over so many years.

Among the giants of theatrical managers, the ones I liked and worked with best were Sam H. Harris, George M. Cohan, Charles and Daniel Frohman, Sam Shubert, and William Morris. They have, unfortunately, gone up the road to follow their fathers.

I believe the greatest acting personalities of my era were John Barrymore—in spite of peeing on my shoes—Gerald du Maurier, Otis Skinner, Jacob Adler, and David Warfield.

My favorite actresses were Alice Brady, Helen Hayes, Laurette Taylor, and Gertrude Lawrence.

The male performers, during my era, who single-handedly were able to hold an audience in the palm of their hand, were Al Jolson going away, then Harry Lauder, Eddie Cantor, Jack Benny, and Ed Wynn. Willie Howard was the best of all the revue comics, bar none.

The stage directors who had it over everyone else were George S. Kaufman, my friend of many years, Arthur Hopkins, Al Lewis, and Jed Harris.

The greatest performers of my time: Charlie—now Sir Charles—Chaplin and Orson Welles, a dear, dear friend for many years.

The finest motion picture director was D. W. Griffith, and the finest motion picture performers: Norma Talmadge, Spencer Tracy, and Mickey Rooney. I also have to reiterate the name of Sir Charles Chaplin as the *greatest* screen performer of all time, bar none.

The best all-around talent in the field of lighter, or "pop," music, Irving Berlin going away. No one will ever be able to match him for his output of hits and all-around good music.

In the past three decades, a performer was not clever enough in the field of business to negotiate the complex deals and contracts necessitated by radio, television, and motion pictures. Therefore, I have to list the best of the "agents," the ten-percenters, who earned every dime of their commission: Abe Lastfogel of William Morris, Charles K. Feldman, Frank Orsatti, Walter Batchelor, Arthur Lyons, Jack Curtis, Max Hart, and Paul Small.

The best of the comics: Milton Berle, Danny Kaye, Jack Haley, Victor Moore, and William Gaxton for the male gender; Ethel Merman and Martha Raye on the distaff side.

My favorite vaudeville acts were McIntyre and Heath, Conn and Corinne, and Smith and Dale.

Among the torch singers of the "good old days," Blossom Seeley ranks number one, followed by Marion Harris and Frances Williams.

As far as nightclub entertainers are concerned, Joe E. Lewis—after he broke away from the Capone mob—was several cuts above everyone else. Then came Harry Richman and Morton Downey. As for the ladies, Sophie Tucker knew what they wanted in the upholstered sewers. Then come Lena Horne, Jane Froman, Beverly Whitney, and for those who liked them stylish, the inimitable Hildegarde.

For whispering into the mike, I always preferred Dinah Shore, Helen Forrest, and Bea Wain.

Among the male crooners: Buddy Clark, Tony Martin, Bing Crosby, and of course, Frank Sinatra, whom I tabbed as a coming star after seeing him perform with Tommy Dorsey at New York's Paramount Theater in the forties.

My list of drama critics who have been the most constructive over the years, as opposed to the destructive critics of today, is headed by George Jean Nathan, the dean of them all, followed by Brooks Atkinson, John Anderson, and Richard Watts. For the amusement business in general, Abel Green of *Variety*.

Among the Broadway columnists who were both good and bad to me, my wives, and my career in general, I have to select Leonard Lyons as the one in closest touch with the people in high places. The most loyal and academic, Louis Sobol. The most picked on, Ed Sullivan. The most debonair, Danton Walker. As for the ladies, Dorothy Kilgallen and her poison pen.

The outstanding newspapermen of my time were Arthur Brisbane, Walter Winchell, Gene Fowler, and Ben Hecht.

My nomination for the most virile and inspiring war correspondent, bar none: Quentin Reynolds.

As for radio sports announcers, which so many of you, unfortunately, probably never heard, and never has there been their equal in authority in front of a microphone: Ted Husing, Bill Stern, Bill Corum, and gravel-voiced Clem McCarthy, who called so many Kentucky Derbies he couldn't count them all.

The baseball personalities of the era, Leo Durocher and Mel Ott; Branch Rickey from the management standpoint.

Sports have never really appealed to me, although I have been a baseball fan for many, many years, ever since I was a bat boy at the Polo Grounds.

I once went to a football game; everyone was getting drunk from pocket flasks, the players would go at it for three minutes and then call a time out. I went home. Of course, the whole world can't be out of step with me, so football must be a great game. It just never appealed to me.

I once started to watch a polo game at Midvale on Long Island and one of the Mdvani brothers was killed in the first two minutes. I went home, got drunk, and never saw another one.

As far as politics are concerned, I believe that a man should be allowed to stay in office until someone better can be found to take his place; the new guy must be better, though.

The most forceful women I have ever met, who were capable of filling almost any man's job, were Madame Chiang Kai-shek, Golda Meir, Mrs. FDR, Edna Ferber, and Sister Kenny.

I have some very definite views on our country; many people have called me a hawk. So be it; they are entitled to their opinions. I still feel we belonged in Vietnam in order to fulfill a commitment to the free world. Because we pulled out when we did, we are now reaping the harvest. As this was written, the forces of North Vietnam are now accomplishing what many years of conflict could not—they are overrunning the South. Can there be anyone who now disagrees with me that we should have remained in South Vietnam—except those, of course, who believe in a Communist-controlled Far East?

The only onstage partner I ever had in show business was Eddie Cantor, my dearly beloved friend of over fifty years. No one has ever been able to replace him in my life—as a friend, a person, or a confidante. It was Eddie who coined the phrase "The March of Dimes" for FDR for his polio campaign funds after Eddie and I had met socially with the president in Warm Springs, Georgia.

I value my friendship with James J. Walker whom I hold in the highest regard. He was handsome, honest, and the finest impromptu public speaker who ever stepped on a podium. Walker was kind and liberal hearted, and when he was the mayor of New York, it was the happiest, gayest city on this earth. Broadway was packed every evening with men resplendent in black ties and dinner jackets, or white ties and capes; the women wore the finest of evening clothes as they made their way into the many theaters in and around Times Square. Following the last-act curtain, they headed for Sardi's, Toots Shor's, and the Rainbow Grill. Nightclubs like the Palais Royal and the Paradise were havens for the sophisticated and mobster alike. There was also Shanley's, where a fellow could bring his girlfriend, his wife, or his mistress and let them dance with Rudolph Valentino or George Burns; or at Murray's Café with Clifton Webb. In later days, there was the great camaraderie that existed at Billy La Hiff's Tavern—later to be immortalized on radio as Duffy's Tavern—the New York Friars Club and the *original* Toots Shor's. In Toots's every night you could see the famed sportswriters of the day lined up along the bar: Grantland Rice, Sid Mercer, Bill Corum, Hype Igoe, the great Jimmy Cannon, with Winchell and Sullivan wandering around. There's nobody around today like that lineup except Jim Murray of the *Los Angeles Times*.

I realize things have changed following World War II, Korea and Vietnam. Nowadays the New York hotel clerks warn you not to walk the streets at night. It used to be so pleasant to wander down Fifth Avenue and window shop at Cartier's, Dunhill, Saks, Bonwit's, and the rest of the fine shops. Columnist Jim Bacon of the *Los Angeles Herald-Examiner* was in New York City three times in three years and was mugged, had his pocket picked, and his hotel room burgled.

You can no longer take a family into Central Park, nor enjoy the beauty and serenity and cozy atmosphere of the Central Park Casino. I think it was Robert Moses who sounded its death knell; he had far too much power. Even the tigers, lions, and the elephants are afraid to go to sleep in the Central Park Zoo come nightfall.

New York was a hap . . . hap . . . happy city when Tammany Hall ran it, though once in a while someone did steal a buck or two when, as the mob would say, "Somebody put their duke in the tambourine."

I still remember when a smart salesman took a prospective buyer to a nightclub in Gotham to see a sparkling show, then known as a cabaret. A great many sales were closed over a bottle of bootlegged bubbly in the happy, exuberant, cosmopolitan atmosphere that was New York in the twenties and thirties. It was easy to do business watching beautiful girls kick their legs high in the air over your head. Forty-second Street used to be the greatest, most exciting thoroughfare in the world, with its Ziegfeld Roof and a dozen or more great and famous theaters, ladies and gentlemen hurrying to the first curtain or to supper somewhere along the way. Now, the inhabitants of Times Square and Forty-second Street look like the latest graduating class from Sing Sing or San Quentin.

I also value my friendship with another great mayor—Samuel Yorty. Sam was feisty, and a lot like Jimmy Walker. Under his twelve-year regime, Los Angeles became one of the greatest cities on earth. Its seaport at Wilmington and the Los Angeles Airport became two of the busiest centers of international transport in the world. Under his administration, the downtown skyline started to match that of New York and is growing every day. There wasn't a city or country in the world that didn't know Sam Yorty and his wife Betts. Sam did more than just travel on the taxpayer; everywhere he went he extolled the virtues of the City of the Angels. He created commerce and encouraged foreign businesses to open branches in Los Angeles to serve the needs of their profit and loss statements—through business available in Los Angeles. He created Sister Cities in the impoverished areas of the world and created tremendous good will. I only hope he is not forgotten. But knowing Sam, I know he won't be.

While on the subject of mayors, the funniest political speech and aftermath I ever heard occurred about ten years ago while I was in Cheyenne, Wyoming, on a USO tour.

A very earnest young man was running for mayor with very little local support or money to finance his campaign. Since the greater part of Cheyenne consists of Indians, he made a speech I witnessed at the local Indian reservation during which he promised the Indians of Wyoming, and particularly Cheyenne, many good things.

After each of the promises, the Indians applauded and there were great shouts of "umm . . . gah, "umm . . . gah." This he interpreted as the Indian version of today's "Right on."

He felt he was "in" from the enthusiastic "umm . . . gahs."

Then the chief took him by the arm. "I want you to see our prize bull. We're very proud of him."

He led the candidate to the corral. "Be careful where you walk around here, I don't want you to step in the umm . . . gah!"

The candidate won the election and kept most of his promises—I found out on another trip to Cheyenne two years later. The way things are going today, most of the politicians on the local, state, and federal level should watch where *they* step; the people are very conscious of "umm . . . gah" today.

Earlier in this account of my life, I mentioned the fact that an engagement at the Hammerstein Theater was very important to a budding vaudevillian—not only for them, but for others as well. Anytime anyone was charged with a sensational crime and released on bail, they would be booked into the Hammerstein for the morbidly curious to view.

Now, instead of being booked into a theater, on the old "Ed Sullivan Show" or the "Tonight Show," they write books and make a fortune; or their lawyers do in lieu of fees.

The taxpayers go to the expense of trying them, incarcerating them in some instances, and the defendants come out of jail and receive upwards of $300,000 advances for the likes of *My Part in the Water Closet Affair*. I believe, to date, some ten books have either been written or contracted for, not to mention Nixon's, on the sordid affair that put this country in such a bad light throughout the world during 1973 and 1974.

There have also been a lot of other books by various murderers and other assorted transgressors of the laws of the land. It would be far better if the money these convicted felons received for their "efforts"—literary and carnal—were returned to the taxpayers by way of paying for their trials and what they cost the country and its citizens. It has always been my understanding that a criminal is not allowed to profit from his crimes—if he's caught.

That doesn't seem to be the case today. . . .

As for future events, I can't help feeling it will be Teddy Kennedy running against either Gerald Ford or Nelson Rockefeller in 1976. Young Kennedy and the rest of the surviving family have far too much ambition and thirst for power for the remaining scion of the Kennedy family to remain a senator from Massachusetts. He may not, in my opinion, be able to win in 1976 because one still cannot gauge the damage Chappaquiddick did to his reputation. In view of the damage caused by Watergate—and the coverup attempt—it may have damaged him irreparably. It also appears that investigative reporters are going to keep digging into Chappaquid-dick from time to time and thus keep the memory alive.

I preferred, a year or so ago, Senator Henry Jackson of Washington—until his ill-advised blast at Henry Kissinger in late 1974.

But only time will tell.

My house in Encino is a virtual museum of awards, trophies, thousands of photographs—most of them of me and the public figures I have mentioned in this account of my life—and many who haven't been mentioned. There are inscribed photographs from Lyndon Johnson, John F. Kennedy, FDR, Eleanor Roosevelt, Sir Winston Churchill, Billy Graham, Generals Arnold and Westmoreland, George M. Cohan, Eddie Cantor, Golda Meir, and David Ben Gurion—everyone, in fact, whose friendship has been part of my life for so many years. On a table just inside my front door there reposes a cane given to me by Harry S. Truman many years ago. I often use it when I have to walk a great deal on my travels, as my left leg still bothers me after I broke it jumping from a burning helicopter in Vietnam thirty feet to the ground. Other occupants of that helicopter weren't so fortunate. I value the Medal of Freedom presented to me by General Ridgeway on the battlefield in Vietnam.

The painting of me as the Immortal Bard hangs over the fireplace with a wicked gleam in my eye as only John Decker could capture it, along with citations, plaques, and awards from every philanthropic and humanitarian organization on whose behalf I have appeared around the world.

But, in a place of honor in my living room reposes what is my proudest award of all—an Oscar presented to me by the Board of Governors of the Academy of Motion Picture Arts and Sciences on April 7, 1970—the Jean Hersholt Humanitarian Award. I knew of the presentation several weeks prior to the ceremony, as it is always announced in advance. I spent many hours working on an acceptance speech to last two minutes; in fact, I spent more time on this one than I usually spend on the half-hour speeches I make two or three times a week.

But when I was called up on the stage of the Dorothy Chandler Pavillion, I could only think of a few of the words:

"God's delay does not mean God's denial."

What else was there to say? The Oscar spoke for itself.

* * *

The preceding has been an honest account of the world I lived in—and hope to live in for many more years. I do not regret one minute of it.

I have been asked many times, if I had it to do all over again, what would I have done differently?

Undoubtedly I would have tried to get an education, which early poverty prevented, and become a lawyer and a politician as my ancestors in England before me.

In spite of everything, though, I am as unashamed of my life as a poodle with a pillow.

EPILOGUE

. . . and It's Not Over Yet

As it was in the beginning, so it is now, at a much slower tempo.

I spend most of my time these days visiting veterans' hospitals entertaining the boys if they can be wheeled into an auditorium. If not, I visit the wards, sit at their bedside, and talk to them. They get little or no entertainment, as our government has almost completely forgotten the USO now that we have no wars raging anywhere in which we are involved—at least at this writing.

Added to that, I'm writing another book, "The Crucifixion of Richard M. Nixon."

As for anything romantic at my time of life, a man must love lightly in self-defense. But who knows what nightfall may bring. A tall brunette who looks part Indian has just entered the Polo Lounge of the Beverly Hills Hotel as I write this Epilogue . . . I'll ask her to have a drink.

The rest?

To be continued . . .

Index